"The Wealth Builder's Handbook A Step-by-Step Guide to Creating Financial Success"

Introduction: Why Wealth Building is Important

Building wealth is essential for achieving financial security and independence. It involves accumulating assets, such as savings, investments, and property, over time to create a stable and sustainable financial future. Here are some of the key reasons why building wealth is important:

1. Provides a safety net: Building wealth provides a safety net against unexpected financial emergencies, such as job loss, medical bills, or home repairs. Having a solid financial foundation allows you to weather these unexpected events without falling into debt or financial hardship.

(1-A) One important benefit of building wealth is that it provides a safety net in case of unforeseen circumstances or emergencies. Life is unpredictable, and unexpected events such as job loss, illness, or accidents can have a significant impact on your financial wellbeing. However, by having a solid financial foundation, you'll be better equipped to weather these storms and come out stronger on the other side.

   - For example, having an emergency fund can help cover unexpected expenses without having to rely on high-interest credit cards or loans. Additionally, having adequate insurance coverage can protect you and your family from financial hardship in case of a medical emergency or other unforeseen circumstances.

   - By building wealth, you can also create a sense of security and peace of mind knowing that you have the resources to take care of yourself and your loved ones in case of a crisis. This can alleviate stress and anxiety, allowing you to focus on more important things in life such as spending time with family, pursuing hobbies, and enjoying your passions.

2. Enables financial freedom: Building wealth enables you to have more control over your life and your choices. You can pursue your passions, take career risks, and make choices that align with your values and goals, without being limited by financial constraints.

 (2-A) Building wealth can also enable financial freedom, which is the ability to live the life you want without being constrained by financial limitations. Financial freedom can mean different things to different people, but generally, it means having the financial resources to do what you want, when you want, without worrying about money.

   - For some people, financial freedom may mean being able to retire early and travel the world. For others, it may mean starting their own business or pursuing their passion without having to worry about the financial implications.

- Whatever your definition of financial freedom may be, building wealth is a key step towards achieving it.

- By building wealth, you can create a passive income stream through investments and other sources of income, allowing you to earn money without having to work for it actively. This can free up your time and allow you to focus on the things that matter most to you.

- Additionally, having financial freedom means that you have the flexibility to make choices based on your values and priorities, rather than being constrained by financial limitations.

- Overall, building wealth can provide a sense of financial security and enable you to live the life you want without being constrained by financial limitations.

3. Builds generational wealth: Building wealth can create a legacy for future generations of your family. It can enable you to leave a financial inheritance or provide educational opportunities for your children or grandchildren.

(3-A) Another important benefit of building wealth is the ability to create generational wealth. Generational wealth is wealth that is passed down from one generation to the next, providing financial security and opportunities for future generations.

- By building wealth through investments, business ownership, and other means, you can create a financial legacy for your children and grandchildren. This can include assets like property, investments, and businesses that can be passed down to future generations.

- Generational wealth can provide a significant advantage to future generations, enabling them to have access to resources and opportunities that may not have been available otherwise. It can also help to break the cycle of poverty and provide a foundation for future success.

Building generational wealth requires a long-term perspective and a commitment to financial planning and management. However, it can be an incredibly rewarding experience to know that you are creating a lasting legacy for your family and future generations.

4. Provides long-term financial security: Building wealth is essential for long-term financial security. It allows you to plan for retirement, cover the costs of education or healthcare, and ensure that you have the resources you need to live a comfortable life as you age.

(4-A) Yes, another key benefit of building wealth is the long-term financial security it provides. By building wealth through savings, investments, and other means, you can create a financial cushion that can help you weather unexpected expenses or economic downturns.

Having financial security can provide peace of mind and reduce stress related to money. It can also provide the freedom to pursue opportunities and take risks without the fear of financial instability.

Building long-term financial security requires discipline, planning, and a long-term perspective. It may involve creating an emergency fund, investing for the future, and reducing debt. However, the rewards of financial security are significant, providing stability and freedom to live life on your own terms.

Overall, building wealth is essential for achieving financial stability, independence, and long-term security. By building wealth, you can create a solid financial foundation that allows you to pursue your passions, achieve your goals, and provide for yourself and your loved ones.

There are several common misconceptions about wealth building that can prevent people from taking action and achieving their financial goals. Here are some of the most common misconceptions:

1. Wealth building is only for the wealthy: Many people believe that building wealth is only possible for those who are already wealthy or who have significant financial resources. However, this is not true. Anyone can build wealth, regardless of their current financial situation. It may require more effort and time, but with the right strategies and mindset, anyone can achieve financial success.

(1-A) This is a common misconception about wealth building, but it is not true. Anyone, regardless of their income or current financial situation, can start building wealth. It is not about how much money you make, but rather about how you manage and grow the money you have.

In fact, building wealth is often more important for those who do not have high incomes or significant assets, as they may not have as many financial resources to fall back on in times of need.

There are many strategies for building wealth, including saving and investing, starting a business, and investing in real estate. With discipline, hard work, and a commitment to ongoing learning and financial education, anyone can begin building wealth and achieving financial security.

2. Wealth building requires taking on significant risk: Some people believe that building wealth requires taking on significant financial risk, such as investing in volatile markets or starting a business with

high overhead costs. While taking risks can be a part of wealth building, it is not the only way to build wealth. There are many low-risk, high-reward investment strategies and business models that can be used to build wealth.

(2-A) While it's true that some wealth building strategies involve taking on more risk than others, not all of them do. For example, saving and investing in a diversified portfolio of stocks and bonds can provide long-term growth potential without significant risk.

Furthermore, there are ways to mitigate risk when investing, such as diversifying your investments, investing in low-cost index funds, and setting stop-loss orders to limit potential losses.

Starting a business or investing in real estate can involve more risk, but with proper planning, research, and management, these strategies can also offer significant rewards.

Ultimately, it's important to weigh the potential risks and rewards of any wealth building strategy and make informed decisions based on your individual financial situation and goals. With the right approach and mindset, it's possible to build wealth without taking on undue risk.

3. Wealth building is a quick fix: Some people believe that building wealth is a quick fix for financial problems, and that it can be achieved overnight. However, building wealth is a long-term process that requires consistent effort and discipline over time. It may take years or even decades to achieve financial independence, but the rewards are well worth the effort.

(3-A) Wealth building is not a quick fix, and anyone who promises fast and easy riches is likely promoting a scam. Building wealth requires discipline, patience, and consistent effort over time. It's important to set realistic goals and understand that wealth building is a marathon, not a sprint.

While some wealth building strategies may offer faster results than others, such as starting a successful business, these still require significant effort and perseverance to achieve. Moreover, building sustainable wealth is not just about making money but also about managing it wisely, minimizing debt, and investing for the long-term.

The key to successful wealth building is to develop a plan that aligns with your goals, establish good financial habits, and stay the course, even when faced with challenges or setbacks. With time, dedication, and a commitment to continuous learning, anyone can build wealth and achieve financial security.

4. Wealth building is only for the young: Some people believe that building wealth is only possible for those who start early in life, and that it is too late for those who have not started building wealth until later in life. However, it is never too late to start building wealth. There are many strategies that can be used to build wealth at any age, and the sooner you start, the more time you have to benefit from the power of compounding.

(4-A) This is a common misconception about wealth building. While it's true that starting early can provide more time to take advantage of compounding interest and investment returns, it's never too late to begin building wealth.

   - In fact, there are several advantages that older individuals may have when it comes to wealth building, such as more experience, greater financial stability, and an established network. Additionally, older individuals may have fewer financial obligations, such as mortgage payments or children's expenses, which can free up resources for saving and investing.

- The key to successful wealth building at any age is to assess your current financial situation, set realistic goals, develop a plan that aligns with your goals, and stay disciplined and committed to your plan over time. It's never too late to start building wealth and securing your financial future.

- Overall, it is important to recognize these misconceptions and to adopt a positive mindset towards wealth building. With the right strategies, discipline, and commitment, anyone can build wealth and achieve financial independence.

"The Wealth Builder's Handbook" is a comprehensive guide to building lasting wealth and achieving financial independence. The book covers a wide range of topics and strategies for building wealth, including:

1. Setting financial goals: This section helps readers identify their financial goals and create a roadmap for achieving them.

(1-A) Setting financial goals is a crucial step in building wealth because it helps you define what you want to achieve and create a plan to get there. Here are some tips for setting effective financial goals:

- Be specific: Set clear and specific goals that are measurable, such as "pay off $10,000 in credit card debt in one year" or "save $20,000 for a down payment on a house within three years."

- Being specific in setting financial goals means defining them with clarity and precision. For instance, instead of setting a general goal of "saving more money," it's better to define a specific amount and a timeframe for saving. For example, "save $10,000 in the next 12 months." This helps to create a clear target and allows for better tracking and measurement of progress. Additionally, being specific with financial goals also means identifying the purpose of the goal, whether it's to pay off debt, buy a house, start a business, or achieve financial independence.

   - Be realistic: Set goals that are achievable based on your current financial situation and resources. It's important to set challenging goals, but they should still be realistic and within reach.

   (1-A1) When setting financial goals, it's important to be realistic. While it's good to aim high and challenge yourself, setting unrealistic goals can lead to frustration, disappointment, and a loss of motivation. Being realistic means setting goals that are achievable based on your current financial situation, income, expenses, and other factors that may impact your ability to achieve your goals. For example, setting a goal to save $50,000 in a year on a $40,000 salary may not be realistic, whereas setting a goal to save $5,000 or 10% of your income may be more achievable. It's important to strike a balance between challenging yourself and setting goals that are within reach.

   - Create a timeline: Set a timeline for achieving your goals, whether it's a short-term goal to be achieved within a few months or a long-term goal that will take several years.

   Creating a timeline is an essential step in achieving your financial goals. It helps you to break down your goals into smaller, actionable steps, and provides a clear roadmap for achieving your objectives. Here is an example of a timeline for achieving a financial goal of saving $10,000 in one year:

   - Month 1-2: Establish a budget and identify areas where you can cut expenses to save money. Create a plan to save $833 per month to reach your goal.

   - Month 3-4: Open a high-yield savings account and set up automatic transfers of $417 every two weeks from your checking account to your savings account.

- Month 5-6: Look for ways to increase your income, such as taking on a side gig or selling unused items. Use the extra income to boost your savings.

- Month 7-8: Evaluate your progress and adjust your plan if needed. Consider making additional cuts to your expenses or increasing your income if you are falling behind.

- Month 9-10: Stay disciplined and continue to save $833 per month. Use visualization techniques to stay motivated and focused on your goal.

- Month 11-12: Celebrate your success! Evaluate what worked well and what didn't during the year, and use these insights to set new financial goals for the future.

(1-E) Prioritize your goals: Determine which goals are most important to you and prioritize them accordingly. This can help you focus your efforts and resources on achieving the most important goals first.

- Prioritizing your financial goals is an important step in achieving them. Here are some tips on how to prioritize your goals:

- Determine the importance of each goal: Think about why each goal is important to you and how it aligns with your overall financial plan. This will help you prioritize your goals based on their level of importance.

- Consider the timeline: Some goals may have a shorter timeline than others. For example, if you want to save for a down payment on a house in the next 3 years, this goal may be a higher priority than saving for retirement, which may have a longer timeline.

- Evaluate the cost: The cost of each goal will also play a role in prioritizing. Goals that require a significant financial investment, such as starting a business or buying a home, may require more focus and resources than goals that have a lower cost, such as building an emergency fund.

   - Consider the potential return on investment: Prioritizing goals with a high potential return on investment may be a wise decision. For example, investing in your education or starting a business may have a high potential return on investment over the long-term.

   - Re-evaluate regularly: Prioritizing goals is not a one-time decision. As your financial situation changes, you may need to re-evaluate and adjust your priorities accordingly.

By prioritizing your financial goals, you can focus your time and resources on the most important goals and increase your chances of achieving financial success.

 (1-F) Review and adjust: Regularly review your goals and progress, and make adjustments as needed. Life circumstances can change, so it's important to stay flexible and adjust your goals and plans accordingly.

   - After setting your financial goals, it's important to regularly review and adjust them as needed. Life circumstances, market conditions, and personal priorities can change over time, and your goals may need to be modified accordingly. You should review your progress towards your goals periodically and make any necessary adjustments to your budget, savings plan, or investment strategy to keep yourself on track. It's also important to celebrate your successes along the way and use them as motivation to keep working towards your financial goals.

Remember, setting financial goals is just the first step. The key to achieving your goals is to develop a plan, stay disciplined, and track your progress over time.

2. Creating a budget: This section provides practical tips and strategies for creating and sticking to a budget that allows readers to save and invest money.

(2-A) Creating a budget is an important step in achieving your financial goals. Here are some steps to follow:

- Track your income: Start by adding up all of your sources of income. This includes your salary, any bonuses or overtime pay, and income from side jobs or investments.

- List your expenses: Next, make a list of all your expenses. This includes everything from fixed expenses like rent/mortgage, utilities, and car payments to variable expenses like groceries, dining out, and entertainment.

- Categorize your expenses: Group your expenses into categories like housing, transportation, food, entertainment, etc.

- Calculate your monthly expenses: Once you've categorized your expenses, add up your total expenses for the month.

- Compare your income and expenses: Compare your total monthly income to your total monthly expenses. If your expenses are greater than your income, you'll need to make some adjustments to your budget.

- Set financial goals: Determine how much you want to save each month and allocate that amount to a specific category in your budget.

- Monitor your budget: Track your spending throughout the month and compare it to your budget. Make adjustments as necessary to stay on track.

Remember, creating a budget is a continual process, and it's important to review and adjust your budget as your financial situation changes.

3. Investing for wealth building: This section covers the basics of investing, including stocks, bonds, and mutual funds, and provides tips and strategies for creating a diversified investment portfolio.

(3-A) Investing is an important component of wealth building as it helps your money grow over time. By investing, you can potentially earn higher returns than you would through saving alone, which can help you reach your financial goals faster.

Here are some key points to consider when investing for wealth building:

- Start early: The earlier you start investing, the more time your money has to grow. Even small amounts invested consistently over a long period of time can add up significantly.

- Diversify your investments: Diversification helps to spread your risk across different types of investments, such as stocks, bonds, and real estate. This can help protect your portfolio against market fluctuations.

- Consider your investment goals and risk tolerance: Your investment strategy should align with your financial goals and your willingness to take on risk. Generally, higher-risk investments may offer higher returns, but may also be more volatile.

- Keep fees and taxes in mind: Fees and taxes can eat into your investment returns over time. Be sure to understand the fees associated with different investment products and consider tax-efficient investment strategies.

- Stay informed: Keep up-to-date with market trends and economic news that may impact your investments. Regularly review your portfolio and make adjustments as needed to stay on track with your goals.

Remember, investing comes with risks, and there are no guarantees of investment returns. It's important to carefully consider your investment options and seek the advice of a financial professional if needed.

4. Real estate investing: This section covers the basics of real estate investing, including rental properties, flipping houses, and investing in REITs.

(4-A) Real estate investing is a popular strategy for building wealth. It involves buying, managing, and selling properties for profit. Real estate can provide a steady stream of passive income, tax benefits, and potential appreciation in value. There are different ways to invest in real estate, including owning and renting out properties, flipping houses, investing in real estate investment trusts (REITs), and more.

Before investing in real estate, it's important to do your research and understand the risks involved. You need to consider factors such as location, market trends, financing options, and property management. It's also important to have a solid understanding of the legal and regulatory requirements of real estate investing.

Real estate can be a complex and demanding investment, but with careful planning and research, it can be a lucrative strategy for building long-term wealth.

5. Building passive income streams: This section covers various ways to create passive income streams, including rental income, dividends, and royalties. (Such as this book)

(5-A) Building passive income streams can be a great way to supplement your primary income and work towards building wealth. Passive income refers to earnings generated from investments or assets that require minimal effort to maintain. Here are some ideas for building passive income streams:

- Rental properties: Owning rental properties can generate a steady stream of income in the form of rent payments. Once you've purchased and set up your rental property, you can hire a property management company to take care of the day-to-day tasks of managing the property.

- Dividend-paying stocks: Investing in dividend-paying stocks can provide a regular stream of income. Dividends are payments made by a company to its shareholders, typically on a quarterly basis.

- Peer-to-peer lending: Peer-to-peer lending platforms allow you to invest in loans made to individuals or small businesses. You earn interest on the loans you fund, which can provide a passive income stream.

- Creating digital products: Creating digital products like ebooks, courses, or software can generate passive income if you can successfully market and sell your products.

- Investing in real estate investment trusts (REITs): REITs are companies that own and manage real estate properties. By investing in a REIT, you can earn a share of the company's profits from its real estate holdings.

Remember that building passive income streams typically requires some upfront effort and investment, but can provide long-term benefits in terms of building wealth and financial independence.

6. Starting a business: This section provides practical tips and strategies for starting a successful business, including identifying a niche, creating a business plan, and marketing your product or service.

(6-A) Starting a business can be a great way to build wealth, create a flexible lifestyle, and make a difference in your community. Here are some steps to consider when starting a business:

- Identify a need or problem in your community that you can solve with a product or service.

- Conduct market research to determine if there is demand for your product or service.

- Develop a business plan that outlines your vision, mission, and strategies for success.

- Choose a legal structure for your business, such as a sole proprietorship, partnership, LLC, or corporation.

- Register your business with the appropriate government agencies and obtain any necessary licenses and permits.

- Secure financing for your business, either through personal savings, loans, or investors.

- Build a team of employees, contractors, or advisors to support your business.

- Develop a marketing plan to promote your business and attract customers.

- Launch your business and continue to refine your strategies based on customer feedback and market trends.

   - Maintain accurate financial records and monitor your progress towards achieving your business goals.

Starting a business can be challenging, but with the right preparation and mindset, it can be a rewarding and fulfilling experience.

7. Building a financial team: This section covers the importance of building a financial team, including a financial advisor, accountant, and attorney, to help you achieve your financial goals.

 (7-A) Building a financial team is an important aspect of wealth building. While it's possible to manage your finances on your own, having a team of professionals can help ensure that you make the best decisions for your financial future.

Here are some members that you may want to consider including on your financial team:

   - Financial advisor: A financial advisor can help you create a comprehensive financial plan, provide investment advice, and help you make important financial decisions.

   - Tax professional: A tax professional can help you navigate the complexities of the tax code, ensure that you're taking advantage of all available tax deductions and credits, and help you plan for future tax liabilities.

   - Attorney: An attorney can help you create and review legal documents such as wills, trusts, and powers of attorney. They can also provide legal advice on various financial matters.

- Accountant: An accountant can help you with bookkeeping, financial statement preparation, and tax planning and preparation.

- Insurance agent: An insurance agent can help you find the right insurance policies to protect your assets and manage your risk.

- Real estate professional: If you're interested in real estate investing, a real estate professional can help you find and evaluate properties, negotiate deals, and manage your rental properties.

- Business consultant: If you're starting a business, a business consultant can help you with everything from developing a business plan to marketing and sales.

When building your financial team, it's important to choose professionals who are experienced, knowledgeable, and trustworthy. You should also make sure that the members of your team work well together and have a shared commitment to helping you achieve your financial goals.

8. Planning for retirement: This section provides tips and strategies for planning for retirement, including creating a retirement plan, maximizing retirement savings, and creating a retirement income stream.

(8-A) Planning for retirement is an essential part of wealth building. It involves preparing for the future by setting aside a portion of your income and investing it to build a nest egg that will provide for you in your retirement years. Retirement planning typically involves identifying your retirement goals, estimating your retirement expenses, determining your retirement income sources, and creating a plan to bridge the gap between your retirement income and expenses.

There are several retirement planning options available, including employer-sponsored retirement plans like 401(k)s and pension plans, as well as individual retirement accounts (IRAs) and annuities. It's important to understand the tax implications and investment options of each type of retirement account, as well as the rules for withdrawals and required minimum distributions.

It's also important to regularly review and adjust your retirement plan as your life circumstances change. This includes revisiting your retirement goals, adjusting your retirement savings rate, and reassessing your investment portfolio to ensure it is aligned with your retirement goals and risk tolerance.

Overall, "The Wealth Builder's Handbook" provides readers with a comprehensive guide to building lasting wealth and achieving financial independence. The book provides practical tips and strategies that can be applied at any stage of life, from starting out in your career to planning for retirement. By following the advice and tips provided in the book, readers can create a solid financial foundation that allows them to pursue their passions, achieve their goals, and provide for themselves and their loved ones.

Chapter 2: Assessing Your Current Financial Situation

Assessing your current financial situation is a critical first step towards building wealth and achieving financial independence. Here are some key factors to consider when assessing your current financial situation:

1. Income: The first step is to understand your current income and how much money you are bringing in each month. This includes your salary, any bonuses or commissions, and any other sources of income.

(1-A) Income refers to the money earned by an individual or entity through work, investments, or other sources. It is generally measured in a specific period, such as a month or a year, and can be classified as gross income or net income. Gross income is the total amount earned before any deductions or taxes are taken out, while net income is the amount remaining after deductions for taxes and other expenses. Income can come from various sources, including wages, salaries, bonuses, dividends, interest, rent, and capital gains.

2. Expenses: The next step is to understand your current expenses and how much money you are spending each month. This includes your rent or mortgage, utilities, groceries, transportation, entertainment, and any other regular expenses.

(2-A) Expenses refer to the costs incurred in the process of generating income. These are the money spent on various goods and services, such as housing, transportation, food, clothing, healthcare, entertainment, and more. Expenses can be classified into fixed expenses and variable expenses. Fixed expenses are recurring expenses that are usually the same every month, such as rent or mortgage payments, while variable expenses fluctuate depending on the usage or consumption, such as utilities or groceries. Understanding and managing expenses is crucial in creating a budget and achieving financial goals.

3. Debt: It is important to understand how much debt you currently have and the interest rates you are paying. This includes credit card debt, student loans, car loans, and any other outstanding debts.

(3-A) Debt refers to money that is borrowed and needs to be repaid with interest. Debt can include credit card balances, personal loans, car loans, student loans, and mortgages. While taking on some debt can be necessary and even beneficial for achieving certain financial goals, such as buying a home or obtaining an education, too much debt can be a major hindrance to wealth building. High levels of debt can lead to high interest payments, which can make it difficult to save and invest for the future. It is important to manage debt carefully and avoid taking on more debt than you can realistically afford to repay.

4. Savings: It is important to understand how much savings you have and whether you have an emergency fund in place. This includes any money you have saved in a savings account, investment accounts, or retirement accounts.

(4-A) Savings are the portion of your income that you set aside for the future. It is the money that you don't spend on immediate expenses but keep aside for long-term goals such as emergencies, retirement, or major purchases like a car or a house. Savings can also serve as a buffer against unexpected expenses or a sudden loss of income.

There are different types of savings, including short-term savings, such as an emergency fund or a rainy-day fund, and long-term savings, such as retirement savings. Short-term savings are typically kept in liquid accounts, such as savings accounts or money market accounts, while long-term savings are often invested in stocks, bonds, or other assets that have the potential to grow in value over time. The amount of money you save each month depends on your income, expenses, and financial goals.

5. Credit score: Your credit score is an important factor in your financial situation, as it can affect your ability to obtain credit, such as loans and credit cards. It is important to understand your current credit score and any factors that may be affecting it.

(5-A) A credit score is a numerical representation of an individual's creditworthiness, based on their credit history. It is used by lenders to assess the likelihood that a borrower will repay their debts on time. Credit scores range from 300 to 850, with higher scores indicating better creditworthiness. A credit score is based on factors such as payment history, credit utilization, length of credit history, types of credit, and recent credit inquiries. A good credit score can help individuals obtain loans and credit cards with favorable terms and lower interest rates. It is important to monitor and maintain a good credit score to ensure financial stability and access to credit when needed.

Once you have assessed your current financial situation, you can begin to develop a plan for building wealth and achieving your financial goals. This may involve creating a budget, reducing expenses, paying off debt, increasing savings, and investing in assets that can generate long-term wealth. By taking control of your financial situation and developing a plan for building wealth, you can achieve financial security and independence over time.

Setting financial goals is a critical step in building wealth and achieving financial independence. Here are some tips for setting effective financial goals:

1. Be specific: Set clear and specific goals that are measurable and attainable. For example, instead of setting a goal to "save money," set a goal to save a specific amount of money each month.

(1-A) Being specific means identifying exactly what you want to achieve with your financial goals. For example, instead of setting a general goal like "save more money," a specific goal would be "save $5,000 for a down payment on a house within the next 12 months." Being specific helps you create a more concrete plan and measure your progress towards achieving your goal.

2. Prioritize your goals: Determine which financial goals are most important to you and prioritize them accordingly. This may include saving for a down payment on a house, paying off debt, or building a retirement fund.

(2-A) Prioritizing your financial goals involves deciding which goals are most important and allocating your resources accordingly. This means identifying your short-term, medium-term, and long-term goals and determining which ones are the most pressing or have the greatest impact on your overall financial well-being.

For example, if you have high-interest credit card debt, paying that off should be a top priority before allocating resources to other financial goals like saving for a down payment on a house or investing for retirement.

Similarly, if you have a young child, saving for their college education may be a higher priority than saving for your own retirement. Prioritizing your goals helps you stay focused and make progress towards achieving them in a meaningful way.

3. Set deadlines: Set specific deadlines for achieving your financial goals to help you stay on track and motivated. For example, if you want to save $10,000 for a down payment on a house, set a deadline of 2 years to achieve that goal.

(3-A) Setting deadlines is a key component of goal setting. It helps create a sense of urgency and accountability, which can increase motivation and likelihood of success. When setting deadlines, it's important to make sure they are realistic and achievable. Break down larger goals into smaller, more manageable steps, and assign deadlines for each step along the way. Consider using a planner or calendar to track your progress and keep yourself on schedule. Remember to be flexible and adjust your deadlines as needed, especially if unforeseen circumstances arise.

4. Break down your goals: Break down larger financial goals into smaller, more manageable steps. This can make your goals feel less overwhelming and more achievable. For example, if your goal is to pay off $20,000 in credit card debt, break it down into a series of smaller goals, such as paying off $5,000 over the next 6 months.

(4-A) Breaking down your goals is an effective way to make them more manageable and easier to accomplish. Here are some steps you can take to break down your goals:

  - Divide your goal into smaller tasks: Take your big goal and break it down into smaller, more manageable tasks. For example, if your goal is to save $10,000 in a year, break it down into smaller savings goals for each month.

  - Set deadlines for each task: Assign a specific deadline for each task to keep you on track.

  - Determine the resources you need: Identify the resources you need to accomplish each task, such as time, money, or skills.

- Take action: Begin working on your tasks and monitor your progress along the way. Celebrate your achievements as you reach each milestone.

- Adjust as needed: Review your progress regularly and adjust your plan as needed. Don't be afraid to change your approach if something isn't working.

By breaking down your goals into smaller steps, you'll be able to focus on achievable tasks and build momentum towards achieving your larger goal.

5. Revisit and adjust your goals regularly: Your financial goals may change over time as your priorities and circumstances change. It is important to regularly revisit and adjust your financial goals as needed to ensure that they remain relevant and achievable.

(5-A) Yes, it is important to regularly review and adjust your financial goals. Life circumstances, financial situations, and priorities can change over time, so it's important to make sure your goals reflect those changes. Regularly revisiting and adjusting your goals can also help you stay motivated and focused on achieving them. It's a good idea to review your goals at least once a year or whenever there is a major change in your life, such as a new job, a change in income, or a major life event.

By setting clear and specific financial goals, prioritizing them, setting deadlines, breaking them down into smaller steps, and revisiting and adjusting them regularly, you can stay on track towards building wealth and achieving financial independence.

Creating a budget is an essential tool for managing your finances and achieving your financial goals. Here are some steps to follow when creating a budget:

1. Track your expenses: Start by tracking all of your expenses for a month, including rent or mortgage payments, utilities, groceries, transportation, entertainment, and any other regular expenses. Use a spreadsheet or a budgeting app to make this process easier.

(1-A) Tracking your expenses is an important part of budgeting and financial planning. By knowing exactly where your money is going, you can identify areas where you might be overspending and make adjustments to stay within your budget. Here are some tips for tracking your expenses:

  - Use a budgeting app: There are many budgeting apps available that can help you track your expenses automatically. Some popular ones include Mint, Personal Capital, and YNAB.

  - Keep receipts and invoices: Whenever you make a purchase, keep the receipt or invoice. This will help you keep track of your expenses and make it easier to categorize them later.

  - Categorize your expenses: Break down your expenses into categories, such as food, housing, transportation, entertainment, etc. This will help you see where your money is going and identify areas where you can cut back.

  - Review your expenses regularly: Set aside time each month to review your expenses and make adjustments to your budget as needed. This will help you stay on track and reach your financial goals.

- Be honest with yourself: Don't try to hide or ignore expenses that you know you shouldn't be making. Be honest with yourself about where your money is going and make changes accordingly.

2. Categorize your expenses: Categorize your expenses into different categories, such as housing, food, transportation, entertainment, and savings.

(2-A) Categorizing your expenses is an important step in tracking your spending and creating a budget. It helps you understand where your money is going and identify areas where you may be overspending.

Here are some common expense categories:

- Housing expenses (rent/mortgage, utilities, maintenance, etc.)

- Transportation expenses (car payments, gas, insurance, maintenance, etc.)

- Food expenses (groceries, dining out, coffee shops, etc.)

- Personal expenses (clothing, grooming, entertainment, hobbies, etc.)

- Debt payments (credit card payments, student loans, etc.)

- Insurance expenses (health, auto, home, etc.)

- Savings and investment expenses (retirement savings, emergency fund contributions, etc.)

- Miscellaneous expenses (gifts, charitable contributions, fees, taxes, etc.)

Categorizing your expenses allows you to see which categories are taking up the largest portion of your budget and make adjustments as needed. It also makes it easier to track your spending over time and see if you are staying within your budget.

3. Determine your income: Calculate your total income, including your salary, any bonuses or commissions, and any other sources of income.

(3-A) To determine your income, you need to calculate all the money you receive during a certain period. This can include:

- Wages or salary from your job.

- Income from self-employment or a business.

- Rental income from property you own.

- Investment income, such as dividends or interest.

- Alimony or child support payments.

- Government benefits, such as Social Security or disability payments.

Add up all of these sources of income to determine your total income for the period. It's important to have an accurate understanding of your income so that you can create a budget and make informed decisions about your finances.

4. Calculate your net income: Subtract your expenses from your income to determine your net income. If your expenses exceed your income, you will need to adjust your budget accordingly.

(4-A) To calculate your net income, you need to subtract your total deductions from your total income. Here are the steps:

- Determine your gross income: This includes your salary or wages, tips, bonuses, and any other income you receive.

- Subtract any pre-tax deductions: These can include contributions to a retirement plan, health insurance premiums, and other pre-tax benefits.

- Subtract any taxes: This includes federal, state, and local taxes that are withheld from your paycheck.

- Subtract any post-tax deductions: These are deductions that are taken out of your paycheck after taxes, such as child support or wage garnishments.

The result is your net income, which is the amount of money you take home after all deductions have been made.

For example, let's say your gross income is $50,000 per year, and you have $5,000 in pre-tax deductions, $8,000 in taxes, and $2,000 in post-tax deductions. To calculate your net income, you would do the following:

$50,000 (gross income) - $5,000 (pre-tax deductions) - $8,000 (taxes) - $2,000 (post-tax deductions) = $35,000 (net income)

5. Set goals: Determine your financial goals, such as paying off debt, saving for a down payment on a house, or building a

retirement fund. Allocate a portion of your income towards these goals.

(5-A) It seems like you have already asked this question before. Nevertheless, setting goals is an essential step in personal finance management. Here are some tips for setting effective goals:

- Be specific: Set clear, well-defined goals that are not open to interpretation.

- Make them measurable: Set goals that you can track and measure over time.

- Make them realistic: Goals should be achievable and not overly ambitious. Unrealistic goals can lead to frustration and disappointment.

- Set a timeline: Give yourself a deadline for achieving your goals. This will help you stay focused and motivated.

- Prioritize: Determine which goals are most important to you and focus on those first.

- Break down larger goals into smaller ones: Breaking down larger goals into smaller, more manageable steps can make them feel less overwhelming and more achievable.

- Revisit and adjust your goals regularly: As your financial situation changes, you may need to adjust your goals to stay on track.

Remember, setting goals is just the first step. It is important to take action and make a plan to achieve those goals.

6. Make adjustments: Review your budget regularly to see if you are on track and make adjustments as needed. This may include cutting

back on discretionary expenses or finding ways to increase your income.

(6-A) Once you have tracked your expenses and income and set your financial goals, it's time to make adjustments. If you find that you are spending more than you are earning, you may need to cut back on some of your expenses or find ways to increase your income.

- Here are some steps you can take to make adjustments:

- Review your expenses: Look at each category of your expenses and identify areas where you can cut back. For example, you may be able to reduce your entertainment expenses or find ways to save on groceries.

- Increase your income: Consider ways to increase your income, such as taking on a side job or asking for a raise at work. You could also consider selling items you no longer need or renting out a spare room.

- Create a new budget: Based on your review of your expenses and income, create a new budget that reflects your revised goals and priorities.

- Monitor your progress: Keep track of your expenses and income on a regular basis to ensure that you are staying on track. If you find that you are not meeting your goals, revisit your budget and make additional adjustments as needed.

Remember, making adjustments to your budget is a normal part of the process. The key is to be flexible and willing to make changes as your financial situation evolves.

Creating and sticking to a budget can help you manage your finances more effectively, reduce stress, and achieve your financial goals. By tracking your expenses, categorizing them, determining your income, setting goals, and making adjustments as needed, you can develop a budget that works for you and helps you achieve financial independence.

Chapter 3: Saving and Investing for the Future

Saving and investing for the future is an important step towards building wealth and achieving financial independence. Here are some tips for saving and investing effectively:

1. Set savings goals: Determine how much money you want to save and by when. This could include creating an emergency fund with three to six months of living expenses, saving for a down payment on a home, or building a retirement fund.

(1-A) Setting savings goals is an important part of building wealth. It allows you to establish a clear objective and work towards it in a systematic manner. Here are some steps to help you set effective savings goals:

- Determine your current financial situation: This involves taking a look at your income, expenses, debts, and any other financial obligations you have.

- Decide on your financial priorities: Once you have a clear idea of your financial situation, you can decide which goals are most important to you. This may involve saving for retirement, building an emergency fund, paying off debt, or investing in a new business venture.

- Create a budget: To achieve your savings goals, you will need to create a budget that reflects your income and expenses. This will help you identify areas where you can cut back on spending and free up more money for saving.

- Set specific savings targets: Once you have a clear idea of your financial priorities and budget, you can set specific savings targets. For example, you may want to save 10% of your income each month or save $500 per month towards your emergency fund.

- Track your progress: Regularly tracking your progress towards your savings goals can help keep you motivated and on track. Consider using a savings app or spreadsheet to monitor your savings and make adjustments as needed.

- Revisit and adjust your goals: As your financial situation changes over time, it's important to revisit and adjust your savings goals as needed. This may involve increasing or decreasing your savings targets or shifting your focus to different financial priorities.

2. Create a budget: As discussed earlier, creating a budget is important for managing your finances and determining how much money you can set aside for savings and investments.

(2-A) To create a budget, follow these steps:

- Determine your income: Calculate your net income, which is your income after taxes and other deductions.

- Track your expenses: Keep track of all of your expenses for a month, including rent or mortgage payments, utilities, groceries, transportation, entertainment, and other miscellaneous expenses.

- Categorize your expenses: Organize your expenses into categories, such as housing, food, transportation, entertainment, and other expenses.

- Identify areas to cut back: Review your expenses and identify areas where you can cut back, such as eating out less, shopping for groceries at a discount store, or using public transportation instead of driving.

- Set goals: Determine how much you want to save each month and set a goal for paying off debt, building an emergency fund, or saving for a specific purchase.

- Make adjustments: Adjust your budget as needed to stay on track with your goals. Consider using budgeting tools and apps to help you stay organized and on track.

3. Start small and be consistent: It's important to start saving and investing as early as possible, even if it's a small amount. Consistency is key - even small contributions made regularly can add up over time.

(3-A) Starting small and being consistent is a key principle in building wealth. Wealth building is a journey that requires patience, discipline, and consistency. It's important to start small and gradually increase your efforts over time.

- For example, if you're starting to save for retirement, you might begin by saving a small percentage of your income each month. As your income grows, you can increase your savings rate. The key is to be consistent and make savings a habit.

- The same principle applies to investing. It's important to start with a small amount of money and gradually increase your investments over time. This will help you to develop good habits and avoid taking on too much risk too quickly.

- The key to success is to stay focused on your goals and keep moving forward, even if progress is slow at first. Over time, small steps can lead to significant progress and wealth building.

4. Consider different types of savings and investment accounts: There are a variety of savings and investment accounts available, each with different benefits and risks. These may include savings accounts, CDs, money market accounts, stocks, bonds, mutual funds, and exchange-traded funds (ETFs).

(4-A) When it comes to saving and investing, there are several different types of accounts to consider. Here are a few common ones:

- Savings accounts: A basic savings account is a good place to start saving money, as it is generally low risk and easily accessible.

- Checking accounts: While not traditionally considered a savings account, a checking account can still be a good option for those who want easy access to their money.

- Certificates of deposit (CDs): CDs are a type of savings account that typically offer a higher interest rate than traditional savings accounts in exchange for locking up your money for a set period of time.

- Individual Retirement Accounts (IRAs): An IRA is a retirement account that allows you to save for retirement with tax advantages. There are two main types of IRAs: traditional and Roth.

- 401(k) plans: If your employer offers a 401(k) plan, it is a good idea to take advantage of it, as it allows you to save for retirement with tax advantages.

- Brokerage accounts: Brokerage accounts are a type of investment account that allows you to invest in stocks, bonds, mutual funds, and other securities.

It's important to research and compare the different types of accounts to determine which ones best meet your needs and financial goals.

5. Diversify your investments: Diversification is important for managing risk in your investment portfolio. Consider investing in a mix of stocks, bonds, and other assets to help spread out risk.

(5-A) Diversifying your investments means spreading your money across different types of assets and investments, such as stocks, bonds, real estate, and commodities, to minimize the risk of losing all of your money if one investment performs poorly. By diversifying, you can potentially maximize returns and reduce overall risk. It's important to keep in mind that diversification doesn't guarantee a profit or eliminate the risk of investment losses, but it can help to manage risk and balance your portfolio.

Here are some ways to diversify your investments:

- Invest in different asset classes: This means allocating your investments across different types of assets, such as stocks, bonds, real estate, and commodities.

- Invest in different sectors: Within each asset class, there are different sectors, such as technology, healthcare, and consumer goods. Investing in a variety of sectors can help to spread risk.

- Invest in different regions: Investing in different regions or countries can help to spread risk and take advantage of growth opportunities in different parts of the world.

   - Use different investment vehicles: You can diversify by investing in different types of investment vehicles, such as mutual funds, exchange-traded funds (ETFs), and individual stocks and bonds.

   - Consider alternative investments: Alternative investments, such as hedge funds, private equity, and real estate, can offer diversification benefits and potentially higher returns, but they also come with greater risk and may not be suitable for all investors.

6. Rebalance your portfolio regularly: It's important to periodically review and rebalance your investment portfolio to ensure it aligns with your financial goals and risk tolerance.

 (6-A) Rebalancing your portfolio means adjusting the allocation of your assets to maintain the desired level of risk and return. Over time, market movements and changes in the value of your investments can cause your portfolio to become unbalanced. Rebalancing helps you to manage risk and ensure that your portfolio stays aligned with your goals.

   - To rebalance your portfolio, you will need to assess your current asset allocation and compare it to your target allocation. If your current allocation is significantly different from your target allocation, you may need to sell some assets and buy others to bring your portfolio back into balance.

   - Rebalancing can be done on a set schedule, such as quarterly or annually, or it can be triggered by specific events, such as a change in your financial situation or a significant market movement. It's important to review your portfolio regularly and adjust your asset allocation as needed to ensure that it remains aligned with your goals and risk tolerance.

7. Seek professional advice: If you're not sure where to start, consider consulting with a financial advisor who can help you develop a savings and investment plan that aligns with your goals.

(7-A) Yes, seeking professional advice is an important part of managing your finances and investments.
   - Financial advisors can provide personalized guidance and help you create a comprehensive financial plan that aligns with your goals and risk tolerance.

   - They can also help you make informed decisions about your investments, manage your portfolio, and adjust your strategy as needed.

   - It's important to do your research and choose a reputable and qualified advisor who has your best interests in mind.

   - Additionally, you should be proactive in communicating with your advisor and regularly reviewing your portfolio and financial plan together.

By setting savings goals, creating a budget, starting small and being consistent, considering different types of savings and investment accounts, diversifying your investments, rebalancing your portfolio regularly, and seeking professional advice as needed, you can effectively save and invest for the future and achieve your financial goals.

There are several types of savings accounts that you can use to save money and earn interest. Here are some common types of savings accounts:

1. Traditional savings account: A traditional savings account is offered by most banks and credit unions. It typically has a low minimum balance requirement and earns interest on the balance in the account.

(1-A) A traditional savings account is a type of bank account where you can deposit money and earn interest on your savings.

- These accounts are typically offered by banks and credit unions, and they provide a safe and secure place to store your money while also earning a small amount of interest.

- One of the main advantages of a traditional savings account is that it is FDIC-insured, which means that your deposits are protected up to $250,000 per depositor, per insured bank. This makes traditional savings accounts a very safe place to store your money.

- However, one of the disadvantages of traditional savings accounts is that they typically offer very low interest rates, which may not keep pace with inflation. This means that the purchasing power of your money may actually decrease over time.

Traditional savings accounts are best suited for short-term savings goals or for emergency funds, where you need quick access to your money and are not as concerned about earning high returns.

2. High-yield savings account: A high-yield savings account typically offers a higher interest rate than a traditional savings account. However, it may require a higher minimum balance or have other restrictions.

(2-A) A high-yield savings account is a type of savings account that typically offers a higher interest rate than a traditional savings account.

- The higher interest rate is usually offered in exchange for a higher minimum deposit or balance requirement, or for other restrictions, such as limits on withdrawals or transfers.

- High-yield savings accounts are often offered by online banks or credit unions and can be a good option for individuals who want to earn a higher return on their savings while keeping their money easily accessible.

3. Money market account: A money market account is a type of savings account that typically offers higher interest rates than traditional savings accounts. It also usually has a higher minimum balance requirement and may have some limitations on withdrawals.

(3-A) A money market account is a type of savings account offered by banks and credit unions. It typically pays a higher interest rate than a traditional savings account and offers some limited check-writing privileges.

- Money market accounts are FDIC-insured, meaning that the funds in the account are protected up to the maximum amount allowed by law.

- Money market accounts are generally considered to be a low-risk investment option, although they may have higher minimum balance requirements and more restrictions on withdrawals than a traditional savings account.

- They are also subject to certain federal regulations, such as a limit on the number of withdrawals or transfers that can be made each month.

4. Certificate of deposit (CD): A CD is a type of savings account that typically offers a higher interest rate than a traditional savings account or money market account. It requires you to deposit a certain amount of money for a set period of time, typically ranging from a few months to several years.

(4-A) A Certificate of Deposit (CD) is a savings instrument offered by banks and credit unions that allows you to invest a specific amount of money for a predetermined period of time at a fixed interest rate.

- CDs typically offer higher interest rates than traditional savings accounts, and the longer the term, the higher the interest rate.

- CDs are considered a safe investment because they are FDIC insured up to $250,000 per depositor per insured bank. However, unlike a traditional savings account, you cannot withdraw funds from a CD penalty-free until the maturity date, which can range from a few months to several years.

- CDs may be a good option for individuals who have a specific savings goal in mind and do not need immediate access to their funds. However, it is important to consider the interest rate and the length of the term when choosing a CD, as early withdrawal penalties can eat into your earnings.

5. Individual Retirement Account (IRA): An IRA is a type of savings account that allows you to save for retirement while earning interest

and potentially reducing your taxes. There are two main types of IRAs: traditional and Roth.

(5-A) An Individual Retirement Account (IRA) is a type of retirement account that allows individuals to save for retirement with tax-free growth or on a tax-deferred basis. There are two main types of IRAs: Traditional and Roth.

- A Traditional IRA allows individuals to make tax-deductible contributions to their retirement savings, which can lower their taxable income in the year the contributions are made.

- The funds in the account grow tax-deferred, which means the account owner will not pay taxes on the growth until they withdraw the money in retirement.

- A Roth IRA is funded with after-tax dollars, so contributions are not tax-deductible. However, the money in the account grows tax-free and withdrawals in retirement are also tax-free.

- Both types of IRAs have contribution limits and penalties for withdrawing money before age 59 1/2, with some exceptions.

- IRAs can be a valuable tool for retirement savings, but it's important to consult with a financial advisor to determine the best strategy for your individual needs and goals.

When choosing a savings account, consider factors such as interest rates, fees, minimum balance requirements, and withdrawal limitations. It's also a good idea to compare different account options and shop around for the best rates and terms.

Investing in stocks, bonds, and mutual funds are common ways to grow your money over the long term. Here's a brief overview of each:

1. Stocks: A stock represents ownership in a company. When you purchase a stock, you are buying a small piece of ownership in the company. Stocks can be bought and sold on stock exchanges such as the New York Stock Exchange (NYSE) or Nasdaq. Stocks are considered a higher risk investment because their value can fluctuate greatly in the short term. However, they may offer greater potential for growth over the long term.

(1-A) Stocks represent ownership in a publicly traded company. When you purchase a stock, you become a shareholder in that company and have the potential to receive a share of its profits through dividends or through the appreciation of the stock's value.

- Stocks are a popular investment option because they offer the potential for high returns over the long term, but they can also be risky and volatile in the short term. It's important to do your research and understand the company and the broader market before investing in stocks.

2. Bonds: A bond is essentially an IOU from a borrower to a lender. When you purchase a bond, you are lending money to an organization, such as a government or corporation. In return, you receive interest payments on the bond and the return of your principal investment when the bond matures. Bonds are considered lower risk investments than stocks because they typically have a fixed interest rate and a predetermined maturity date.

(2-A) Bonds are a type of fixed-income investment that involve lending money to a company or government entity in exchange for regular interest payments and eventual return of the principal investment.

- When you purchase a bond, you are essentially loaning money to the issuer, who promises to pay you interest on a regular basis (usually twice a year) and return the full amount of your investment when the bond matures.

- Bonds can be issued by governments (treasury bonds), corporations (corporate bonds), or municipalities (municipal bonds), and can range in duration from short-term (less than one year) to long-term (up to 30 years or more).

- Bonds are generally considered less risky than stocks, but offer lower potential returns.

3. Mutual funds: A mutual fund is a type of investment that pools money from many investors to purchase a diversified mix of stocks, bonds, and other assets. Mutual funds are managed by professional investment managers who make investment decisions on behalf of the fund's investors. By investing in a mutual fund, you are able to diversify your investments across a variety of assets and reduce risk.

(3-A) A mutual fund is a type of investment vehicle that pools money from multiple investors to purchase securities such as stocks, bonds, or other assets. Mutual funds are managed by professional fund managers who use the pooled money to construct a portfolio of investments that aligns with the fund's investment objectives.

- When you invest in a mutual fund, you own a portion of the overall fund, and the value of your investment rises or falls with the performance of the underlying assets in the portfolio.

- Mutual funds are a popular investment choice because they offer investors access to a diversified portfolio of investments, even with a relatively small amount of money.

- Additionally, mutual funds are easy to buy and sell, and many funds offer low fees and expenses. There are many types of mutual funds, including index funds, actively managed funds, and exchange-traded funds (ETFs).

   - Each type of fund has its own benefits and drawbacks, so it's important to research and understand the options available before investing.

When investing in stocks, bonds, or mutual funds, it's important to consider your risk tolerance and investment goals. It's also important to do your research and understand the investment options available to you. Consider seeking the advice of a financial advisor or investment professional if you are unsure about how to invest your money.

Creating an investment portfolio involves choosing a mix of investments that align with your financial goals and risk tolerance. Here are some steps to follow when creating an investment portfolio:

1. Determine your investment goals: Identify why you are investing and what you hope to achieve. Are you investing for retirement, a down payment on a home, or to build wealth over the long term?

   (1-A) Before making any investment, it is important to determine your investment goals. This will help you determine the type of investment that is right for you and how much risk you are willing to take on. Some common investment goals include:

   - Capital appreciation: This is the goal of increasing the value of your investment over time.

- Income generation: This is the goal of generating a regular stream of income from your investments.

- Wealth preservation: This is the goal of protecting your wealth by investing in low-risk, stable assets.

- Speculation: This is the goal of taking on high-risk investments in the hopes of earning a large return.

Once you have determined your investment goals, you can start to research different types of investments that align with your goals and risk tolerance. It is important to remember that all investments carry some level of risk, so it is important to diversify your portfolio and consult with a financial advisor if you are unsure about the right investment strategy for you.

2. Assess your risk tolerance: Consider how much risk you are willing to take on. Generally, investments that offer higher returns, such as stocks, also come with higher risk. Investments that are lower risk, such as bonds, typically offer lower returns.

(2-A) Assessing your risk tolerance is an important step in determining your investment strategy. It involves understanding how much risk you are willing to take in pursuit of potentially higher returns. Here are a few factors that can influence your risk tolerance:

- Age: Generally, the younger you are, the more risk you can afford to take since you have a longer time horizon to ride out any market volatility.

- Financial situation: If you have a stable job and adequate emergency savings, you may be more comfortable taking on higher risk investments.

- Investment goals: Your investment goals, such as saving for retirement or a down payment on a house, can help determine your risk tolerance.

- Personality: Some people are naturally more risk-averse than others, while others may be comfortable taking on more risk.

It's important to note that risk tolerance is personal and subjective, and there is no one-size-fits-all approach. Understanding your risk tolerance can help you make informed investment decisions that align with your goals and financial situation.

3. Choose your asset allocation: Decide how much of your portfolio you want to allocate to different asset classes, such as stocks, bonds, and cash. Your asset allocation should align with your investment goals and risk tolerance.

(3-A) Asset allocation refers to the way you divide your investments among different asset classes such as stocks, bonds, and cash equivalents. The percentage of each asset class in your portfolio is known as your asset allocation.

- Your asset allocation should be based on your investment goals, time horizon, and risk tolerance.

- When choosing your asset allocation, it's important to consider your investment goals. If your goal is long-term growth, you may want to consider a higher allocation to stocks. If you're more interested in preserving your capital, you may want a higher allocation to bonds.

- Your risk tolerance is also an important consideration. If you have a high risk tolerance, you may be comfortable with a higher allocation to stocks. If you have a low risk tolerance, you may prefer a higher allocation to bonds.

   - Ultimately, your asset allocation should be diversified, meaning you have exposure to different types of investments within each asset class. This can help reduce your overall investment risk.

4. Choose specific investments: Once you have determined your asset allocation, choose specific investments to include in your portfolio. Consider factors such as diversification, fees, and performance history.

 (4-A) When choosing specific investments, it's important to consider your investment goals, risk tolerance, and asset allocation. Here are some common types of investments to consider:

   - Stocks: These are shares of ownership in a company. They offer the potential for high returns but also come with high risk.

   - Bonds: These are loans made to a company or government in exchange for interest payments. They are generally considered less risky than stocks, but offer lower returns.

   - Mutual funds: These are a collection of stocks, bonds, and other securities that are managed by a professional fund manager. They offer instant diversification and are a good option for beginner investors.

   - Exchange-traded funds (ETFs): These are similar to mutual funds, but trade on an exchange like a stock. They offer diversification and low fees.

   - Real estate: This includes investment properties, REITs (real estate investment trusts), and crowdfunding platforms. Real estate investments offer the potential for passive income and long-term appreciation.

- Alternative investments: This includes commodities, currencies, and hedge funds. These investments are generally more complex and risky, and should only be considered by experienced investors.

It's important to do your research and choose investments that align with your goals and risk tolerance. Consider seeking advice from a financial professional before making any investment decisions.

5. Rebalance your portfolio: Regularly review your portfolio and rebalance it as needed to maintain your desired asset allocation.

(5-A) Rebalancing your portfolio is an important step in managing your investments. Over time, the value of each investment in your portfolio will change, and this can throw off your desired asset allocation. Rebalancing involves selling some investments and buying others in order to bring your portfolio back in line with your target asset allocation.

- For example, suppose you have a target asset allocation of 60% stocks and 40% bonds. If your stocks perform well over the course of a year, the value of your stock holdings may increase to 70% of your portfolio, while the value of your bond holdings decreases to 30%. To rebalance your portfolio, you would sell some of your stocks and use the proceeds to buy more bonds, bringing your asset allocation back to 60/40.

- Rebalancing helps you to maintain the level of risk that you are comfortable with and can help to ensure that your portfolio remains diversified. It is recommended that you rebalance your portfolio at least once a year, although you may choose to do it more often if you prefer.

It's important to remember that investing involves risk and there is no guaranteed return. Consider seeking the advice of a financial advisor or investment professional when creating an investment portfolio. They can help you make informed investment decisions based on your unique financial situation and goals.

Compound interest is a powerful tool that can help you grow your money over time. It is the interest earned on both the principal amount and the interest that has accumulated over time. Here's an example of how compound interest works:

Let's say you invest $10,000 in an account that earns 5% interest per year. After the first year, you would earn $500 in interest, bringing your total account balance to $10,500. In the second year, you would earn 5% interest on $10,500, which is $525. So at the end of the second year, your total account balance would be $11,025. Over time, the interest earned on the interest you've already earned can add up significantly.

The key to harnessing the power of compound interest is to start investing early and allow your money to grow over a long period of time. The longer your money is invested, the more time it has to compound and grow.

Here's an example to illustrate this point: Let's say you start investing $100 per month at age 25 and continue to do so until age 65. Assuming an average annual return of 7%, your investment would grow to over $200,000 by the time you retire. However, if you wait until age 35 to start investing the same amount, your investment would only grow to around $100,000 by the time you retire.

In summary, compound interest is a powerful tool that can help you grow your money over time. Starting early and investing regularly can help you take advantage of this powerful concept and achieve your financial goals.

Chapter 4: Building Wealth Through Entrepreneurship

Entrepreneurship can be a powerful way to build wealth over time. Here are some steps to consider when building wealth through entrepreneurship:

1. Identify a need in the market: Look for opportunities to create a product or service that fills a need in the market. This could be something completely new, or an improvement on an existing product or service.

(1-A) Identifying a need in the market involves researching and analyzing consumer demand for a particular product or service. This may involve studying market trends, examining consumer behavior, and identifying gaps in the market where existing products or services do not meet the needs or wants of customers.

Some ways to identify a need in the market include:

   - Conducting market research: This involves gathering data on customer needs, preferences, and behavior through surveys, focus groups, or online research.

- Examining existing products and services: By analyzing existing products or services in a particular market, it may be possible to identify gaps or areas where improvements could be made to better meet consumer needs.

- Analyzing trends: By tracking trends in consumer behavior or industry developments, it may be possible to anticipate new needs or demands in the market.

- Listening to feedback: Feedback from customers, industry experts, or other stakeholders can be a valuable source of information on unmet needs or areas where improvements could be made.

- Brainstorming: Brainstorming sessions with a team or other stakeholders can be a useful way to generate ideas for new products or services that meet specific customer needs.

2. Create a business plan: Develop a solid business plan that outlines your goals, target market, pricing strategy, marketing plan, and financial projections. A well-crafted business plan can help you secure funding and stay on track as you grow your business.

(2-A) Creating a business plan is an essential step in starting a new business. A business plan helps you clarify your business idea, set realistic goals, and create a roadmap for achieving those goals. Here are some key elements to include in your business plan:

- Executive summary: This section should briefly describe your business idea, your target market, and your goals.

- Company description: This section should provide more detail about your business, including its legal structure, location, and history (if applicable).

- Market analysis: This section should provide an overview of your target market and its needs, as well as an analysis of your competition.

- Products and services: This section should describe what you will be selling, how it will benefit your customers, and how you plan to market it.

- Marketing and sales: This section should describe your marketing and sales strategies, including how you will reach your target market, what channels you will use, and how you will measure your success.

- Operations: This section should describe how you plan to run your business, including your staffing and management structure, your production processes, and any suppliers or vendors you will work with.

- Financial projections: This section should include financial forecasts for your business, including projected revenue, expenses, and profits.

- Funding requirements: This section should describe how much money you need to start and run your business, and how you plan to obtain that funding.

- Milestones and metrics: This section should outline specific goals and objectives for your business, as well as how you plan to measure your progress toward those goals.

Remember, your business plan is a living document, and you should update it regularly as your business evolves. A solid business plan can help you secure funding, attract customers, and ultimately build a successful business.

3. Secure funding: Depending on the size and scope of your business, you may need to secure funding from outside investors or lenders. This could include traditional bank loans, crowdfunding, or venture capital.

(3-A) Securing funding is an essential part of starting a business. It involves identifying the amount of money needed to start and run the business and finding the most suitable funding sources.

Here are some common funding sources for small businesses:

- Personal savings: Many entrepreneurs use their personal savings to fund their business ventures.

- Friends and family: Some entrepreneurs receive funding from their friends and family members.

- Bank loans: Business owners can apply for loans from traditional banks or credit unions.

- Small Business Administration (SBA) loans: The SBA offers several loan programs to help small businesses.

- Crowdfunding: Crowdfunding platforms such as Kickstarter, Indiegogo, and GoFundMe allow entrepreneurs to raise money from a large number of people.

- Angel investors: Angel investors are wealthy individuals who invest in startups in exchange for an equity stake.

- Venture capitalists: Venture capitalists are investors who provide funding to startups with high growth potential in exchange for an equity stake.

- Grants: Some government agencies and private organizations offer grants to small businesses.

It's important to remember that each funding source has its advantages and disadvantages. Entrepreneurs should carefully evaluate their options and choose the funding sources that best fit their needs and goals.

4. Build a team: As your business grows, you will need to build a team of talented and motivated individuals who can help you achieve your goals. Look for people who share your vision and bring unique skills and perspectives to the table.

(4-A) Building a team is an essential part of starting and running a successful business. Here are some key steps to building a team:

- Determine your needs: Before you can build a team, you need to determine the roles and responsibilities necessary for your business. Identify what skills and experience are required for each position.

- Develop job descriptions: Develop job descriptions that outline the responsibilities and qualifications required for each position. This will help you attract the right candidates for each role.

- Recruit candidates: Once you have identified the roles you need to fill and developed job descriptions, you can start recruiting candidates. You can use job boards, social media, and your network to find potential candidates.

- Conduct interviews: Conduct interviews with the candidates you have selected. Ask open-ended questions to learn about their experience, skills, and work style.

- Check references: Before making an offer, check the candidate's references to ensure they have the necessary skills and experience.

- Make an offer: Once you have selected a candidate, make them an offer that includes their salary, benefits, and any other relevant details.

- Onboard your team: Once your team is in place, you will need to onboard them. This includes providing them with the tools and resources they need to be successful in their roles.

- Provide ongoing support: Provide your team with ongoing support to help them succeed. This includes providing feedback, training, and resources to help them develop their skills and grow in their roles.

- Foster a positive culture: Foster a positive culture that supports and encourages your team. This includes recognizing their contributions, providing opportunities for growth, and creating a collaborative and supportive environment.

5. Focus on customer satisfaction: In order to build a successful business, you need to focus on delivering high-quality products or services and providing exceptional customer service. This will help you build a loyal customer base and drive repeat business.

(5-A) Focusing on customer satisfaction is key to the success of any business. When customers are satisfied with a business, they are more likely to return and make additional purchases, and they may also recommend the business to others. Here are a few ways to focus on customer satisfaction:

- Listen to your customers: Ask for feedback and actively listen to their responses. This can help you understand what they like about your business, as well as areas where you can improve.

- Provide excellent customer service: Train your employees to be friendly, helpful, and responsive to customers' needs. Make sure customers can easily reach you through multiple channels, such as phone, email, and social media.

   - Offer quality products or services: Make sure your products or services are of high quality and meet or exceed customer expectations. This can help you build a loyal customer base.

   - Be transparent: Communicate openly and honestly with your customers. If there are any issues, address them promptly and take steps to resolve them.

   - Reward loyalty: Offer promotions, discounts, or other incentives to reward customers who make repeat purchases or refer others to your business. This can help build customer loyalty and keep them coming back.

6. Continuously innovate and improve: As you grow your business, it's important to stay on top of industry trends and continuously innovate and improve your products or services. This will help you stay ahead of the competition and maintain your market share.

 (6-A) Continuous innovation and improvement are crucial for the success and longevity of any business. As the market and customer needs evolve, businesses must adapt and improve their products, services, and operations to stay relevant and competitive.

Here are some ways businesses can continuously innovate and improve:

   - Gather feedback from customers: Regularly collecting feedback from customers can help businesses identify areas for improvement and develop new products or services that meet their needs.

   - Stay up-to-date with industry trends: Staying informed about the latest trends and technological advancements in the industry can help businesses identify new opportunities for growth and innovation.

   - Invest in research and development: Allocating resources to research and development can help businesses create new products or services and improve existing ones.

   - Foster a culture of innovation: Encouraging employees to share their ideas and experiment with new approaches can help businesses stay ahead of the curve.

   - Monitor and measure performance: Regularly tracking and analyzing key performance indicators can help businesses identify areas for improvement and measure the impact of new initiatives.

   - By continuously innovating and improving, businesses can stay relevant, attract and retain customers, and maintain a competitive edge in the marketplace.

Building wealth through entrepreneurship requires hard work, perseverance, and a willingness to take risks. However, with the right strategy and execution, entrepreneurship can be a powerful way to achieve your financial goals and build long-term wealth.

Starting a business can offer a wide range of benefits, including:

1. Unlimited earning potential: Unlike working for someone else, starting a business allows you to set your own income potential. If you are successful, there is no limit to how much money you can make.

(1-A) The term "unlimited earning potential" typically refers to the idea that there is no upper limit to the amount of money one can earn in a particular field or industry.

- It implies that with hard work, dedication, and skill, an individual can earn as much as they desire.
- However, it's important to note that while some industries or professions may have a higher earning potential than others, there are often factors such as market conditions, competition, and personal circumstances that can affect an individual's earning potential.

2. Flexibility and freedom: As a business owner, you have the freedom to set your own schedule and work on your own terms. This can allow you to achieve a better work-life balance and spend more time with your family and pursuing your passions.

(2-A) Flexibility and freedom are some of the benefits of starting your own business. As a business owner, you have the flexibility to set your own schedule and work from anywhere.

- You also have the freedom to make your own decisions and pursue your passion. This allows you to create a work-life balance that works for you and your family.

- Additionally, starting a business can offer the opportunity to work with like-minded individuals and build a team that shares your vision and goals.

3. Personal fulfillment: Starting and growing a successful business can be incredibly rewarding and provide a sense of personal fulfillment. You have the opportunity to create something from

scratch and make a positive impact on your community and customers.

(3-A) Starting and running your own business can bring a great deal of personal fulfillment. As an entrepreneur, you have the opportunity to turn your passions and interests into a viable business that can benefit others.

- You also have the ability to make decisions that align with your personal values and beliefs. This can lead to a greater sense of purpose and satisfaction with your work.

- Additionally, as you see your business grow and succeed, it can be incredibly rewarding and fulfilling to know that you played a major role in its success.

4. Building equity: As your business grows and becomes more profitable, you are building equity in the company. This can provide a valuable asset that can be sold or used to secure loans in the future.

(4-A) Building equity refers to increasing the value of an asset, such as a property or investment, over time through various means, such as paying down a mortgage, making improvements to the property, or earning a return on an investment.

- Equity can be an important aspect of wealth building, as it represents the portion of the asset that belongs to the owner and can be used to build further wealth or as collateral for other investments.
- Building equity can take time and effort, but can ultimately lead to increased financial stability and opportunities for growth.

5. Control over your future: By starting a business, you are taking control of your financial future and creating a legacy for yourself and your family. You are not reliant on an employer or the job market for your livelihood.

(5-A) Having control over your future is a potential benefit of building wealth. When you have financial stability, you have more options and freedom in your life.

- You can make choices about your career, where you live, and how you spend your time without being solely driven by financial considerations.

- Building wealth can give you a sense of security and the ability to plan for the future, whether that means retiring early, starting a business, or pursuing a passion project.

- Additionally, building wealth can provide a sense of pride and accomplishment in your financial success, which can be personally fulfilling.

6. Learning and growth: Starting a business requires you to continually learn and grow as you face new challenges and opportunities. This can help you develop valuable skills and knowledge that can benefit you in all areas of your life.

(6-A) Starting and running a business can offer numerous opportunities for learning and growth. As a business owner, you'll be required to learn about a variety of topics, such as finance, marketing, sales, operations, and management.

- You'll have to adapt to changing market conditions, technological advancements, and industry trends. You may also have to develop new skills or acquire knowledge in areas you're not familiar with.

- Moreover, running a business can expose you to new experiences and perspectives, broaden your network, and challenge you to think creatively and innovatively.

- You'll be able to learn from your mistakes, develop problem-solving skills, and gain confidence in your abilities.

- Overall, starting and running a business can be a rewarding experience that offers continuous learning and personal growth opportunities.

Overall, starting a business can be a challenging but incredibly rewarding experience that offers a wide range of benefits. With the right strategy and execution, you can achieve your financial goals and build a successful and fulfilling career as a business owner.

Identifying market opportunities is a crucial step in starting a successful business. Here are some tips to help you identify potential opportunities in the market:

1. Look for unmet needs: Look for gaps in the market where there are unmet needs or underserved segments. These gaps could be related to product features, customer service, or pricing.

(1-A) Looking for unmet needs is a great way to identify business opportunities. Start by observing the world around you and considering what problems or frustrations people might have that could be solved by a new product or service.

- You can also conduct market research to gain a deeper understanding of consumer needs and preferences.

   - Additionally, you can brainstorm with others or participate in entrepreneurship programs to generate ideas and develop new products or services.

   - The key is to be creative and open-minded, and to look for gaps in the market that you can fill with a unique solution.

2. Stay up-to-date with industry trends: Keep up with the latest trends in your industry and pay attention to emerging technologies, changes in consumer behavior, and shifts in the competitive landscape. This can help you identify new opportunities and stay ahead of the curve.

(2-A) Staying up-to-date with industry trends is crucial for any business or entrepreneur. It allows you to remain competitive and relevant in your field, anticipate changes and challenges, and take advantage of emerging opportunities. Here are some ways you can stay current with industry trends:

   - Attend industry events and conferences: Attend industry events, such as trade shows and conferences, to network with peers, learn about new products and services, and gain insights from thought leaders.

   - Follow industry publications: Subscribe to industry publications, such as journals and newsletters, to stay informed about the latest news, research, and trends.

   - Use social media: Follow relevant industry leaders, organizations, and hashtags on social media to stay up-to-date with the latest developments and discussions.

   - Conduct market research: Conduct regular market research to identify changes in customer needs, preferences, and behaviors, as well as emerging opportunities and threats.

- Network with peers: Build relationships with peers in your industry to exchange ideas, share best practices, and stay informed about industry trends.

- Hire a consultant: Consider hiring a consultant or expert in your field to provide insights and recommendations based on their experience and expertise.

By staying up-to-date with industry trends, you can position yourself and your business for success and growth.

3. Conduct market research: Conduct market research to gather insights into consumer needs and preferences, as well as the strengths and weaknesses of your competitors. This can help you identify opportunities to differentiate your business and provide unique value to customers.

(3-A) Market research is an essential step in starting and growing a business. It involves gathering information about the market, including competitors, customers, and industry trends, to make informed decisions about your products or services. Here are some steps to conducting effective market research:

- Define your research objectives: Be clear about what you want to achieve with your research. This will help you determine what information you need to gather.

- Identify your target audience: Determine who your ideal customer is and what their needs and preferences are. This will help you tailor your products or services to meet their needs.

- Conduct primary research: This involves gathering firsthand information directly from your target audience. This can be done through surveys, focus groups, or interviews.

- Conduct secondary research: This involves gathering information from existing sources such as industry reports, market studies, and government statistics.

   - Analyze your data: Organize and interpret your data to identify patterns and trends. This will help you make informed decisions about your business.

   - Use your research to make informed decisions: Use the insights gained from your research to make informed decisions about your products or services, marketing strategy, and overall business strategy.

Remember that market research is an ongoing process, and it is essential to stay up-to-date with industry trends and customer preferences to remain competitive in the market.

4. Analyze data: Use data analytics to identify patterns and trends that can help you spot opportunities in the market. This could include analyzing sales data, website traffic, and social media engagement.

 (4-A) Analyzing data is the process of examining information and statistics in order to draw conclusions and insights from the data. It involves collecting, cleaning, processing, and visualizing data to help make informed decisions.

   - When conducting market research or trying to make business decisions, it is important to analyze relevant data to gain a better understanding of the market and consumer behavior.

   - This can include analyzing sales data, consumer feedback, and competitor research.

- Data analysis can help identify trends and patterns that may not be immediately apparent, and can provide insights into customer preferences, market demand, and potential areas for growth. It can also help identify areas of weakness or opportunities for improvement.

  - There are many tools and techniques available for data analysis, including statistical analysis, data visualization, and machine learning.

  - The specific method chosen will depend on the type of data being analyzed and the goals of the analysis.

Ultimately, the goal of data analysis is to provide actionable insights that can inform business decisions and help achieve business goals.

5. Brainstorm with others: Collaborate with colleagues, friends, or other entrepreneurs to brainstorm new ideas and identify potential opportunities. Sometimes, a fresh perspective can help you see things in a new light and identify new opportunities.

 (5-A) Brainstorming with others is a great way to generate new ideas and get feedback on your existing ones. You can bring together a group of people with diverse backgrounds and perspectives to stimulate creative thinking and problem-solving. Here are some tips for effective brainstorming sessions:

  - Set clear goals: Define the purpose and scope of the brainstorming session. Identify specific problems or opportunities you want to address, and make sure everyone is on the same page.

  - Create a comfortable environment: Make sure everyone feels comfortable sharing their ideas. Encourage open communication and active listening. Consider using icebreaker activities or team-building exercises to help people get to know each other and build trust.

   - Use a structured approach: There are many structured brainstorming techniques you can use to facilitate the session, such as mind mapping, SWOT analysis, or the Delphi method. Choose a method that suits your goals and team dynamics.

Encourage creativity: Encourage everyone to think outside the box and challenge assumptions. Avoid judgment or criticism of ideas during the session. Instead, focus on building on each other's ideas and generating new ones.

   - Capture and organize ideas: Make sure to capture all the ideas that are generated during the session. Use a whiteboard, flip chart, or digital tool to record them. Once the session is over, organize the ideas into categories or themes and prioritize them based on their potential impact and feasibility.

   - Follow up and take action: After the brainstorming session, make sure to follow up with the team to discuss the ideas further and develop an action plan. Assign responsibilities and set deadlines to ensure that the ideas are implemented.

Remember that identifying market opportunities requires both creativity and strategic thinking. By staying attuned to consumer needs, industry trends, and emerging technologies, you can identify new opportunities and position your business for success.

Writing a business plan is an important step in starting a successful business. Here are the key components that you should include in your business plan:

1. Executive Summary: This is a brief overview of your business plan that should highlight the key elements of your business, including your products or services, target market, and financial projections.

(1-A) An executive summary is a brief and concise summary of a larger document or report, usually written for business or academic purposes.

- It is typically found at the beginning of the document and provides an overview of the main points, including the purpose of the document, the methodology used to gather information, the key findings, and the conclusions or recommendations.

- An executive summary is intended to give readers a quick understanding of the content and significance of the document, without requiring them to read the entire thing.

- It should be well-written, clear, and engaging, and it should be tailored to the intended audience.

- Executive summaries are commonly used in business plans, research reports, grant proposals, and other types of documents.

- They are often the first thing that decision-makers will read, so they are critical to the success of the document as a whole.

2. Company Description: This section should provide a detailed description of your business, including your mission statement, company structure, and history.

(2-A) A company description provides an overview of the business, including its products or services, history, and goals. It should also include information about the industry in which the business operates, the target market, and any competitive advantages or challenges the company faces.

The company description should answer the following questions:

- What products or services does the company offer?
- How long has the company been in business?
- What is the history of the company, including any major milestones or accomplishments?
- What are the goals and objectives of the company?
- What industry does the company operate in?
- Who is the target market for the company's products or services?
- What competitive advantages does the company have?
- What challenges does the company face?

The company description is typically included in the business plan or investor pitch deck and is an important part of introducing the company to potential investors, partners, and customers.

3. Market Analysis: This section should describe your target market, including their needs, demographics, and behavior. It should also include an analysis of your competitors and how you plan to differentiate yourself.

(3-A) Market analysis is a process of gathering and analyzing information about the market in which a business operates. It involves studying the target market, identifying customer needs, and evaluating the competition. The information gathered during market analysis helps businesses to make informed decisions about marketing, sales, and operations.

Some key elements of market analysis include:

- Identifying the target market: The first step in market analysis is to identify the target market for your product or service. This involves analyzing the demographics, psychographics, and behavior of your target customers.

- Understanding customer needs: Once you have identified your target market, you need to understand their needs and preferences. This involves researching their pain points, desires, and expectations.

- Analyzing the competition: Another important aspect of market analysis is analyzing the competition. This involves identifying direct and indirect competitors, analyzing their strengths and weaknesses, and determining how your business can differentiate itself from them.

- Evaluating market trends: Market trends can have a significant impact on your business. By analyzing market trends, you can identify opportunities and potential threats to your business.

- Estimating market size and growth: Understanding the size and growth rate of your target market is essential for making informed business decisions. This involves analyzing data on population, consumer spending, and industry trends.

Overall, market analysis is a critical component of any successful business strategy. By understanding the market and your customers, you can develop effective marketing and sales strategies, identify new opportunities, and differentiate your business from the competition.

4. Products and Services: This section should describe your products or services in detail, including how they will be produced, delivered, and priced.

(4-A) The section of Products and Services in a business plan should describe in detail what the company is selling, how it benefits the customers, and how it differentiates from the competitors. It is essential to provide a clear description of the product or service, including its features and benefits.

- In this section, you should also discuss any intellectual property that you own or plan to file, such as patents, copyrights, and trademarks. This information will help investors understand the uniqueness of your product and what advantages it can bring to the market.

- Additionally, you should provide information about any future products or services that your company may offer. This information can help investors understand the potential growth of your business and your long-term vision.

- When writing about products and services, it is crucial to focus on the benefits that they bring to the customers. Make sure to describe how your products or services solve a specific problem or meet a particular need.

Providing customer testimonials or reviews can also be helpful to show potential investors that your product or service has been well-received by the market.

5. Marketing and Sales Strategy: This section should describe how you plan to market and sell your products or services, including your advertising and promotional strategies.

(5-A) Marketing and sales strategy is an essential part of any business plan. This section should outline how you plan to promote and sell your products or services to your target market. Here are some key elements to consider when developing your marketing and sales strategy:

- Define your target market: Identify the specific group of people or businesses that are most likely to buy your products or services. Consider factors like age, income level, location, and interests to create a detailed customer profile.

- Develop your unique value proposition: Determine what makes your products or services unique and why customers should choose your business over competitors.

- Choose your marketing channels: Consider a variety of channels to reach your target market, such as social media, email marketing, advertising, or direct mail. Choose the channels that are most effective for your target market and budget.

- Develop your sales strategy: Determine how you will sell your products or services, such as through an online store, physical location, or a combination of both. Consider pricing strategies, payment options, and customer service policies.

- Measure your success: Establish metrics to track the success of your marketing and sales efforts. Consider factors like website traffic, conversion rates, customer feedback, and sales revenue.

Remember to regularly evaluate and adjust your marketing and sales strategy based on data and customer feedback to ensure ongoing success.

6. Operations Plan: This section should describe how your business will operate on a day-to-day basis, including your staffing and management structure, production process, and facilities.

(6-A) An operations plan is a document that outlines how a business will run its operations to achieve its goals. It covers all aspects of the business, including production, delivery, staffing, and logistics. An operations plan should provide a roadmap for the company to achieve its strategic objectives by defining the processes and procedures that will be used to deliver products and services. The plan should also provide metrics to measure the effectiveness of the processes and procedures.

Some of the key components of an operations plan include:

- Production plan: This section should outline how the company will produce and deliver its products or services. It should include details about the production process, the equipment and materials needed, and the timelines for delivery.

- Staffing plan: This section should outline how the company will staff its operations. It should include details about the skills and experience needed for each position, as well as the number of employees needed.

- Logistics plan: This section should outline how the company will manage its inventory, supply chain, and shipping operations. It should include details about the suppliers, transportation methods, and warehousing facilities that will be used.

- Quality control plan: This section should outline how the company will ensure the quality of its products or services. It should include details about the quality control processes that will be used, as well as the metrics that will be used to measure the effectiveness of these processes.

- Risk management plan: This section should outline how the company will manage risk in its operations. It should include details about the potential risks and how they will be mitigated.

Overall, an operations plan should be a detailed document that outlines how the company will deliver its products and services. It should be regularly reviewed and updated to ensure that it remains effective and relevant to the company's operations.

7. Financial Plan: This section should include your financial projections, including your income statement, cash flow statement, and balance sheet. It should also include a detailed analysis of your startup costs and funding requirements.

(7-A) The financial plan is an important section of a business plan that details the financial projections and strategies for the business. It includes information about the startup costs, operating expenses, revenue projections, cash flow analysis, and funding requirements.

The financial plan should include the following components:

- Startup Costs: This includes all the costs associated with starting the business, such as equipment, inventory, legal fees, and marketing expenses.

- Sales Forecast: This section should outline the projected sales for the business over a certain period, typically 3-5 years. This should include the pricing strategy, sales channels, and customer segments.

- Profit and Loss (P&L) Statement: The P&L statement shows the revenue and expenses for the business over a certain period, typically 3-5 years. This helps to determine the profitability of the business.

- Cash Flow Analysis: This section outlines the cash flow projections for the business, including the inflow and outflow of cash. It helps to determine the cash needs of the business and when additional funding may be required.

- Break-Even Analysis: This section helps to determine the sales volume required to cover the business's fixed and variable costs.

This helps to determine the minimum sales volume required for the business to break even.

   - Funding Requirements: This section outlines the funding required to start and grow the business. It should include details about the sources of funding, such as loans, equity, or grants.

   - Financial Assumptions: This section outlines the assumptions made in the financial projections, such as the growth rate, interest rates, and inflation rates.

The financial plan should be based on realistic assumptions and should be regularly reviewed and updated as the business grows and evolves. It is important to ensure that the financial projections are accurate and achievable to avoid overestimating revenue or underestimating expenses, which could lead to financial difficulties for the business.

8. Appendix: This section should include any additional information that is relevant to your business plan, including resumes of key staff members, legal documents, and marketing materials.

   (8-A) The appendix of a business plan is an optional section that includes additional materials that support the main content of the plan.

   - It may include things like resumes of key team members, detailed financial projections, legal documents, marketing research data, and more.

   - The purpose of the appendix is to provide readers with supplementary information that they can reference if they need more detail or context about a particular aspect of the business plan.

- It is important to note that the appendix should only include relevant and necessary materials, as including too much extraneous information can detract from the overall impact of the business plan.

Remember, a well-written business plan can help you attract investors, secure financing, and guide your business towards success. Be sure to take the time to research and carefully craft each section of your business plan to ensure that it accurately represents your business and positions it for growth.

Launching and growing a successful business takes hard work, dedication, and a solid strategy. Here are some key steps to help you build and grow your business:

1. Develop a strong brand: Your brand is what sets you apart from your competitors and communicates your unique value proposition to your customers. Focus on creating a strong brand identity, including your company name, logo, tagline, and messaging.

(1-A) Developing a strong brand can help your business stand out from competitors, build customer loyalty, and create a memorable image in the minds of your target audience. Here are some steps to develop a strong brand:

- Define your brand: Start by determining your brand's mission, values, and unique selling proposition (USP). This will help you create a clear and consistent message that resonates with your audience.

- Know your audience: Understand your target audience's needs, values, and interests. This will help you create messaging and visuals that resonate with them.

- Develop a visual identity: Create a logo, color palette, and typography that represent your brand's personality and values. These elements should be consistent across all marketing materials and communications.

- Create a brand voice: Develop a tone of voice that aligns with your brand's personality and values. This will help you create consistent messaging across all touchpoints.

- Build a strong online presence: Create a website and social media accounts that align with your brand's visual identity and messaging. Regularly post content that showcases your brand's personality, values, and products or services.

- Foster brand loyalty: Create a positive customer experience that aligns with your brand's values. This will help you build a loyal customer base that advocates for your brand.

- Continuously evaluate and evolve: Regularly evaluate your brand's performance and adjust your messaging, visuals, and tone of voice as needed to stay relevant and resonant with your target audience.

2. Build a strong online presence: In today's digital age, having a strong online presence is essential for success. Build a user-friendly website, create engaging social media profiles, and use search engine optimization (SEO) strategies to increase your visibility online.

(2-A) Building a strong online presence is essential for any business in today's digital age. Here are some steps you can take to create a strong online presence:

- Build a website: Your website is your online storefront, and it's often the first impression potential customers have of your business.

Make sure your website is easy to navigate, visually appealing, and provides all the necessary information about your business.

- Create valuable content: Creating valuable and relevant content can help establish you as an authority in your industry and improve your search engine rankings. This content can be in the form of blog posts, videos, infographics, and more.

- Use social media: Social media platforms such as Facebook, Twitter, and Instagram are powerful tools for reaching new customers and engaging with your existing audience. Use these platforms to share your content, promote your products or services, and interact with your followers.

- Utilize search engine optimization (SEO): SEO is the process of optimizing your website to improve its visibility and ranking on search engines like Google. This involves optimizing your website's content, metadata, and backlinks to improve your ranking for relevant search terms.

- Use email marketing: Email marketing is a great way to stay in touch with your customers and keep them informed about new products or services, promotions, and other updates. Make sure your emails are relevant, valuable, and provide clear calls to action.

- Monitor and respond to online reviews: Online reviews can greatly influence a potential customer's decision to do business with you. Make sure to monitor and respond to both positive and negative reviews, and use them to improve your products or services.

By following these steps, you can build a strong online presence and attract new customers to your business.

3. Develop a marketing strategy: A strong marketing strategy can help you reach your target audience and generate sales. Identify your target audience, create a messaging strategy, and use a mix of online and offline marketing tactics to reach your audience.

(3-A) Developing a marketing strategy involves identifying your target audience, determining your unique selling proposition (USP), and creating a plan to reach and engage your audience. Here are some steps to consider when developing a marketing strategy:

- Define your target audience: Who is your ideal customer? What are their demographics, interests, and pain points? Understanding your target audience will help you create messages that resonate with them.

- Determine your USP: What makes your product or service unique? Why should someone choose you over your competitors? Your USP should be a key component of your messaging.

- Conduct market research: Use surveys, focus groups, and other research methods to better understand your target audience and competition. This will help you identify areas of opportunity and refine your marketing messaging.

- Set marketing goals: What do you want to achieve through your marketing efforts? This could include increasing brand awareness, generating leads, or driving sales.

- Choose marketing channels: There are many marketing channels to choose from, including social media, email marketing, content marketing, search engine optimization (SEO), and advertising. Determine which channels will be most effective for reaching your target audience.

- Create a content calendar: Plan out your content and promotions in advance. This will help ensure that you have a consistent message and that you are staying on track with your marketing goals.

   - Implement and monitor your strategy: Execute your marketing plan, track your results, and adjust your strategy as needed. Regularly reviewing and updating your marketing plan will help you stay ahead of the curve and achieve your goals.

4. Build a strong team: As your business grows, it's important to build a strong team of employees who are aligned with your company's vision and values. Focus on hiring talented, motivated individuals who can contribute to the success of your business.

  (4-A) Building a strong team is crucial for the success of any business. Here are some tips for building a strong team:

   - Hire the right people: Take the time to find people who are a good fit for your company culture and who have the skills and experience needed for the job.

   - Provide clear job descriptions: Make sure each team member knows their role and what is expected of them.

   - Encourage open communication: Foster an environment where team members feel comfortable sharing their thoughts and ideas.

   - Provide ongoing training and development: Offer opportunities for team members to learn new skills and grow in their careers.

   - Reward and recognize team members: Show your appreciation for your team members' hard work and contributions.

   - Foster a positive work environment: Make sure your workplace is a supportive and positive environment where team members feel valued and respected.

- Set clear goals: Make sure everyone on the team understands the company's goals and how their work contributes to those goals.

- Encourage collaboration: Encourage team members to work together and share ideas to achieve common goals.

- Lead by example: Set a positive example for your team by being a good role model and demonstrating the behavior you want to see in your team members.

- Provide opportunities for feedback: Regularly solicit feedback from your team members to learn how you can improve as a leader and how you can better support your team.

5. Monitor and adjust your strategy: As your business grows, be sure to monitor your progress and adjust your strategy as needed. Use analytics tools to track your key performance indicators (KPIs) and adjust your marketing, sales, and operations strategies as needed.

(5-A) Once you have developed a marketing strategy and implemented it, it's important to continuously monitor and adjust it as needed. This can help ensure that you are reaching your target audience effectively and that your efforts are producing the desired results.

- One way to monitor your strategy is to track your key performance indicators (KPIs) such as website traffic, social media engagement, and sales conversions. Regularly reviewing your KPIs can help you identify areas of success and areas that may need improvement.

- Additionally, stay up-to-date with industry trends and your competition. This can help you adjust your strategy as needed and stay ahead of the curve.

   - Finally, be open to feedback from customers and colleagues. This can help you identify areas for improvement and adjust your strategy accordingly.

6. Focus on customer service: Happy customers are essential for the success of any business. Focus on delivering excellent customer service at every touchpoint, and use customer feedback to continually improve your products and services.

 (6-A) Focusing on customer service is essential for any business. When customers have a positive experience, they are more likely to return and recommend your business to others. Here are some tips for providing excellent customer service:

   - Be responsive: Respond promptly to customer inquiries and concerns, whether it's via phone, email, or social media.

   - Listen actively: Take the time to listen to your customers' needs and concerns. Show them that you value their input and are willing to work with them to find a solution.

   - Be friendly and professional: Always greet customers with a smile and a friendly demeanor. Use professional language and avoid using slang or jargon that customers may not understand.

   - Provide personalized service: Try to personalize your interactions with customers by using their name and taking note of their preferences and past interactions with your business.

   - Go above and beyond: Whenever possible, try to exceed your customers' expectations. This could be something as simple as offering free samples or going out of your way to accommodate a special request.

   - Use feedback to improve: Encourage customers to provide feedback on their experiences with your business. Use this feedback to identify areas where you can improve and make changes as needed.

Remember, good customer service is not just about solving problems and addressing complaints. It's also about creating a positive experience for your customers that will keep them coming back.

7. Continuously innovate: In today's rapidly changing business environment, it's important to continuously innovate and adapt to new trends and technologies. Stay up-to-date with the latest industry trends and continually look for ways to improve and differentiate your business.

 (7-A) Continuous innovation is an important aspect of business growth and success. It involves developing new and improved products, services, processes, or business models to meet the evolving needs and demands of customers and the market. Here are some tips for continuous innovation:

   - Stay informed about industry trends and emerging technologies: Keep up-to-date with the latest trends and technologies in your industry by attending conferences, reading industry publications, and networking with other professionals.

   - Encourage creativity and idea generation: Encourage your team to come up with new ideas and solutions by fostering a culture of creativity, open communication, and collaboration.

- Test and iterate: Test new ideas and innovations in a small-scale environment and iterate based on feedback and results. This allows you to refine your ideas and make improvements before launching on a larger scale.

- Embrace failure: Accept that not every idea or innovation will succeed and be willing to learn from failures and mistakes. Use these experiences to improve and refine future innovations.

- Keep an eye on competitors: Monitor your competitors' innovations and adapt your strategy accordingly to stay ahead of the curve.

- Foster a culture of continuous improvement: Encourage your team to continuously look for ways to improve existing products, services, and processes to better meet customer needs and stay competitive.

Remember, building and growing a successful business takes time and effort. Focus on creating a strong foundation, staying agile and adaptable, and delivering value to your customers at every stage of the customer journey. (Trust Me I Run 3 Businesses As Of Right Now)

Chapter 5: Real Estate Investing

Real estate investing is a popular way to build wealth through the ownership and management of properties. Here are some key steps to help you get started in real estate investing:

1. Determine your investment strategy: Real estate investing can take many forms, including rental properties, fix-and-flip properties, and commercial real estate. Determine which strategy aligns with your goals, financial situation, and expertise.

(1-A) Determine your investment strategy involves identifying your investment goals, assessing your risk tolerance, and choosing appropriate investment options based on those factors.

- Identify your investment goals: Your investment goals may include things like saving for retirement, a down payment on a house, or a child's education. Knowing your investment goals will help you determine your investment time horizon and how much risk you are willing to take on.

- Assess your risk tolerance: Risk tolerance is the amount of risk you are willing to take on in your investments. This will depend on your age, financial situation, investment goals, and personal preferences. Generally, the longer your investment time horizon, the more risk you can afford to take on.

- Choose appropriate investment options: Based on your investment goals and risk tolerance, you can choose appropriate investment options. These may include stocks, bonds, mutual funds, exchange-traded funds (ETFs), or other types of investments.

- Develop a diversified portfolio: Diversification is important in reducing investment risk. You can diversify your portfolio by investing in a variety of asset classes, such as stocks, bonds, and real estate, as well as different industries and geographies.

- Monitor and adjust your portfolio: It's important to regularly monitor your investments and adjust your portfolio as needed to ensure that it aligns with your investment goals and risk tolerance. This may involve rebalancing your portfolio or making changes to your investment strategy.

2. Research potential properties: Once you have determined your investment strategy, research potential properties that align with your goals. Consider factors such as location, market demand, rental income potential, and property condition.

(2-A) Researching potential properties is an important step in the real estate investment process. Here are some tips to help you get started:

 - Determine your investment goals: Before you begin your property search, it's important to determine your investment goals. Are you looking for a property to flip quickly for a profit, or are you looking for a long-term rental property? Knowing your investment goals will help you determine the type of property you're looking for.

 - Research the local real estate market: Researching the local real estate market will give you a better understanding of property values, rental rates, and the demand for rental properties in the area. You can research local real estate market trends online or by speaking with a local real estate agent.

 - Determine your budget: Once you know your investment goals and have researched the local real estate market, you can determine your budget. Determine how much you can afford to spend on a property, taking into account any repairs or renovations that may be necessary.

 - Search for properties: Once you have determined your investment goals, researched the local real estate market, and determined your budget, you can begin searching for properties.

You can search for properties online, through a local real estate agent, or by driving through the neighborhoods you're interested in.

   - Evaluate potential properties: Once you have found potential properties, evaluate them based on your investment goals and budget. Look at the property's location, condition, potential rental income, and any repairs or renovations that may be necessary.

   - Make an offer: If you find a property that meets your investment goals and budget, you can make an offer. Work with a local real estate agent to make an offer that is fair and reasonable.

   - Close the deal: If your offer is accepted, you can close the deal. Work with a real estate attorney to ensure that all of the necessary paperwork is completed and that the transaction is legally binding.

3. Secure financing: Real estate investing typically requires a significant amount of capital, so it's important to secure financing before making an offer on a property. Consider options such as traditional mortgages, private lenders, or partnerships with other investors.

 (3-A) When it comes to investing in real estate, securing financing is a critical step. Here are some ways to secure financing for your real estate investment:

   - Traditional lenders: You can consider approaching traditional lenders such as banks, credit unions, or mortgage companies to obtain a mortgage for your investment property.

   - Hard money lenders: Hard money lenders are private individuals or companies that offer short-term loans with higher interest rates and fees compared to traditional lenders.

- Crowdfunding: Crowdfunding is a way to pool funds from multiple investors to finance a real estate project.

- Owner financing: Owner financing is when the seller finances the sale of the property, and you make payments to the seller over time, rather than obtaining a traditional mortgage.

- Partnerships: You can consider partnering with another investor to secure financing for your real estate investment.

It's important to do your research and consider all options before selecting a financing method that works best for your investment goals and financial situation.

4. Make an offer and close the deal: Once you have identified a property and secured financing, make an offer and negotiate the terms of the deal. Work with a real estate attorney or agent to ensure that all legal requirements are met and the deal is closed successfully.

(4-A)Once you have found a suitable property, you can make an offer to the seller. Your offer should be based on the property's fair market value, as well as any repairs or renovations that may be needed. You may also want to include contingencies in your offer, such as a home inspection or financing contingency.

- If the seller accepts your offer, you will need to sign a purchase agreement and provide a deposit. Your next steps will depend on the specific details of the purchase agreement, such as the closing date and any other conditions that must be met before closing.

- At closing, you will sign all of the necessary paperwork and pay any remaining costs associated with the purchase. This may include closing costs, property taxes, and any other fees or charges associated with the transaction.

- Once the closing is complete, you will become the legal owner of the property. Congratulations!

5. Manage the property: If you are investing in a rental property, it's important to manage the property effectively to maximize your returns. This may include tasks such as tenant screening, property maintenance, and rent collection.

(5-A) Managing a property is a critical aspect of real estate investment. Here are some key steps to follow:

- Hire a property manager: You can choose to manage your property yourself, but it's a good idea to hire a property manager if you don't have the time or expertise to handle all aspects of property management. A property manager can help you with tasks such as finding tenants, collecting rent, handling repairs, and dealing with legal issues.

- Set rent rates: Before renting out your property, you need to set competitive rent rates. This involves researching the local real estate market to determine what other landlords are charging for similar properties.

- Advertise your property: To attract tenants, you need to market your property effectively. You can use a variety of methods to advertise your property, including online listings, classified ads, and yard signs.

- Screen tenants: Finding the right tenants is crucial for a successful rental property. You can use various screening techniques such as background checks, credit checks, and employment verification to ensure you choose responsible tenants who will pay rent on time and take good care of your property.

- Collect rent: Collecting rent is an essential part of managing a rental property. You need to establish clear payment policies, set up a system for collecting rent, and enforce penalties for late payments.

Handle repairs and maintenance: You are responsible for maintaining the property and handling repairs when necessary. This includes fixing plumbing issues, addressing electrical problems, and performing routine maintenance tasks.

- Stay compliant with regulations: There are numerous legal and regulatory requirements that you need to comply with when managing a rental property. For example, you need to follow local zoning laws, ensure your property meets safety standards, and comply with fair housing regulations.

- Keep accurate records: It's essential to keep accurate records of all financial transactions related to your rental property. This includes rent payments, expenses, and taxes.

- Plan for unexpected expenses: Property management comes with unexpected expenses. You should set aside a reserve fund to handle unexpected repairs or other emergencies.

By following these steps, you can effectively manage your rental property and maximize your return on investment.

6. Monitor your investment: As with any investment, it's important to monitor your real estate investment and make adjustments as needed. Track your rental income, expenses, and cash flow, and adjust your management strategy as needed to optimize your returns.

(6-A) Monitoring your real estate investment is crucial to its long-term success. Here are some things to consider:

- Rental Income: Keep track of your rental income and ensure that it is sufficient to cover your expenses, including mortgage payments, property taxes, and maintenance costs.

- Vacancy Rate: Monitor the vacancy rate of your property and take steps to keep it rented. Consider hiring a property manager to help you find and retain tenants.

- Property Maintenance: Regularly inspect your property to identify any maintenance needs. Promptly address any issues to prevent them from becoming major problems.

- Market Trends: Stay up-to-date on the real estate market in your area. Be aware of trends in rental rates, property values, and other factors that may impact your investment.

- Financing: Regularly review your financing options and consider refinancing if it makes sense for your situation.

- Insurance: Ensure that your property is adequately insured and review your policy regularly to ensure that it meets your needs.

- Tax Implications: Consult with a tax professional to understand the tax implications of your investment and ensure that you are taking advantage of all available deductions.

By regularly monitoring your investment, you can make informed decisions and take action to ensure its long-term success.

Remember, real estate investing can be a lucrative way to build wealth, but it also carries risks and requires a significant amount of work and expertise. Do your research, work with experienced professionals, and always prioritize sound financial management to increase your chances of success.

Real estate investing offers a variety of advantages, including:

1. Potential for long-term appreciation: Real estate values tend to appreciate over time, which can provide a steady stream of passive income and long-term wealth building.

(1-A) Investing in real estate offers the potential for long-term appreciation, which means that the value of the property may increase over time.

- This can lead to a significant return on investment if the property is held for a long period of time. Additionally, real estate investments can provide a steady stream of passive income through rental income, which can also appreciate over time.

- This makes real estate an attractive option for those looking for a long-term investment with potential for growth.

- However, it's important to keep in mind that real estate values can also decline over time, so it's important to do your research and invest wisely.

2. Cash flow: Rental income from investment properties can provide a steady stream of passive income, which can help offset expenses and generate additional income.

(2-A) Cash flow refers to the money that comes in and goes out of a business or investment over a period of time.

- Positive cash flow means that a business or investment generates more cash than it spends, while negative cash flow means that it spends more cash than it generates.

- Cash flow is important because it helps to ensure that a business or investment has enough money to pay its bills and make investments for growth.

- It also helps investors to evaluate the performance of a business or investment and make informed decisions.

3. Tax benefits: Real estate investing offers a variety of tax benefits, including deductions for mortgage interest, property taxes, and depreciation.

(3-A) Investing in real estate can provide various tax benefits, including:

- Depreciation deductions: Rental property owners can deduct depreciation from their taxable income each year, which reduces their tax liability.

- Mortgage interest deduction: Real estate investors can deduct the interest paid on their mortgage from their taxable income, which also lowers their tax liability.

- Property tax deduction: Investors can also deduct property taxes paid on their investment properties from their taxable income.

- 1031 Exchange: Investors can defer paying taxes on the sale of a property by using a 1031 Exchange, which allows them to reinvest the proceeds in a similar property without recognizing capital gains.

- Deductible expenses: Investors can also deduct various expenses related to their rental property, such as repairs, maintenance, and management fees, from their taxable income.

It is important to consult with a tax professional to fully understand the tax implications of investing in real estate and to ensure compliance with all relevant tax laws and regulations.

4. Diversification: Real estate investing provides a diversification opportunity that can help reduce risk in a broader investment portfolio.

(4-A) Real estate investments can provide diversification in your investment portfolio, which is important for reducing risk.

   - It can help balance out your portfolio and reduce the impact of any one asset class.

   - Additionally, real estate investments have historically shown a low correlation to the stock market, which means that they can provide a level of protection against stock market volatility.

5. Inflation hedge: Real estate values tend to rise with inflation, which can provide a hedge against inflation and help preserve purchasing power.

(5-A) Real estate investment can act as an inflation hedge. Inflation is the rate at which the general level of prices for goods and services is rising and, as a result, the purchasing power of currency is falling.

   - Inflation can have a negative impact on investments such as stocks and bonds because it can decrease the value of future cash flows.

   - Real estate, on the other hand, tends to increase in value in line with inflation, making it a potential hedge against inflation.

- Additionally, rental income from real estate can increase with inflation as landlords can raise rent prices to keep up with rising costs.

6. Control over the investment: Real estate investing provides investors with a level of control over the investment that may not be available with other types of investments.

(6-A) One advantage of real estate investing is the level of control that an investor can have over the investment.

- Unlike some other investment types, real estate allows for direct ownership of a physical asset that can be improved, renovated, and managed in a way that can increase its value and income potential.

- Real estate investors can make decisions about when and how to buy or sell a property, as well as how to manage and maintain it, which can have a significant impact on the success of the investment.

7. Leverage: Real estate investing can be leveraged through the use of financing, which can amplify returns and allow investors to acquire properties that may be out of reach with cash purchases.

(7-A) Leverage refers to the use of borrowed money to invest in an asset or business, with the expectation of generating a greater return than the cost of borrowing. In real estate investing, leverage is commonly used to purchase property, with the expectation that the rental income generated by the property will exceed the cost of the mortgage and other expenses, resulting in a profit for the investor.

- Leverage can magnify returns, allowing investors to generate more income or gain equity faster than they could by using only their own capital.

- However, it also amplifies risk, as losses can also be magnified. In addition, leveraging a property may require a significant down payment and can increase the overall cost of the investment over time due to interest payments.

- It is important for investors to carefully evaluate their risk tolerance and financial situation before using leverage in real estate investing or any other investment strategy.

Remember, real estate investing also carries risks, including market volatility, property management challenges, and unexpected expenses. Careful research, due diligence, and professional advice can help mitigate these risks and increase your chances of success.

There are several types of real estate investments that you can consider:

1. Residential rental properties: Residential properties, such as single-family homes, condos, and apartments, can be rented out to generate rental income.

 (1-A) Residential rental properties are properties that are rented out to tenants as their place of residence. These can include single-family homes, duplexes, townhouses, and apartments.

- Investing in residential rental properties can provide a number of benefits, including:

- Regular income: Rental income from tenants can provide a steady stream of income on a monthly basis.

- Appreciation: As property values increase over time, the value of the property can appreciate, providing a potential source of long-term wealth.

-Tax benefits: There are a number of tax deductions available to real estate investors, including deductions for property taxes, mortgage interest, and depreciation.

- Control over the investment: Investors have control over the property and can make decisions about how to manage and maintain it.

- Inflation hedge: Rental income and property values can rise with inflation, providing a hedge against inflation.

However, investing in residential rental properties also comes with risks, including:

- Vacancies: If tenants move out, the property may be vacant and not generating rental income.

- Maintenance and repairs: Property owners are responsible for maintaining and repairing the property, which can be costly.

- Property management: Property owners may need to hire a property manager to handle tenant relations, rent collection, and maintenance.

- Market fluctuations: Real estate values can fluctuate based on market conditions, and rental income can be affected by changes in demand.

Overall, investing in residential rental properties can be a good option for those looking for long-term income and appreciation, but it requires careful planning and management to ensure a successful investment.

2. Commercial rental properties: Commercial properties, such as office buildings, retail spaces, and warehouses, can be rented out to businesses to generate rental income.

(2-A) Commercial rental properties are a type of real estate investment that involves purchasing and managing commercial properties such as office buildings, retail spaces, industrial properties, and warehouses. The goal of investing in commercial real estate is to generate rental income from tenants and potentially benefit from property appreciation over time.

Investors can benefit from several advantages of investing in commercial rental properties, including:

- Higher potential rental income: Commercial properties typically have higher rental rates than residential properties, providing investors with the potential for higher rental income.

- Long-term lease agreements: Commercial tenants typically sign longer lease agreements than residential tenants, providing investors with a more stable source of rental income.

- Diversification: Investing in commercial rental properties can provide diversification within a real estate portfolio, reducing risk and increasing potential returns.

- Tax benefits: Commercial property owners can take advantage of tax deductions, including depreciation, mortgage interest, and property taxes.

- Appreciation potential: Commercial properties have the potential to appreciate in value over time, providing investors with the opportunity for long-term capital appreciation.

However, investing in commercial rental properties also comes with some potential risks, such as economic downturns, difficulty in finding tenants, and high maintenance costs. It is important for investors to conduct thorough due diligence and work with experienced professionals to mitigate these risks and make informed investment decisions.

3. Fix-and-flip properties: This type of investment involves purchasing a property, renovating it, and then selling it for a profit.

(3-A) Fix-and-flip properties are a type of real estate investment where an investor buys a property, fixes it up, and then sells it for a profit. This type of investment is typically short-term and requires a significant amount of work to renovate the property and increase its value.

- Investors who specialize in fix-and-flip properties often look for properties that are undervalued, in need of repair or renovation, and have the potential to increase in value with improvements. They then purchase the property, make the necessary renovations, and sell it for a profit.

- While fix-and-flip properties can be profitable, they can also be risky. Renovation costs can quickly add up, and unexpected issues can arise during the renovation process.

- Additionally, the real estate market can be unpredictable, which can impact the sale price of the property. As a result, it's important for investors to carefully research the property and the market before investing in a fix-and-flip property.

4. Real estate investment trusts (REITs): REITs are investment vehicles that own and operate income-producing real estate, such

as apartment buildings, office complexes, and shopping centers. Investors can buy shares in a REIT and receive a portion of the income generated by the underlying properties.

(4-A) Real Estate Investment Trusts (REITs) are a type of investment vehicle that pools money from multiple investors to invest in a diversified portfolio of income-generating real estate assets, such as office buildings, apartment complexes, retail spaces, and hotels.

- REITs are required by law to distribute at least 90% of their taxable income to shareholders in the form of dividends, which makes them an attractive investment option for income-seeking investors.

- There are two main types of REITs: Equity REITs and Mortgage REITs. Equity REITs own and manage income-generating real estate properties, while Mortgage REITs invest in mortgage loans and other types of debt securities backed by real estate.

- Investing in REITs provides several benefits, including diversification, liquidity, and the potential for capital appreciation.

- REITs also offer exposure to the real estate market without the need for direct property ownership, which can require significant amounts of time, money, and expertise. However, like all investments, REITs also come with risks, such as interest rate risk, tenant default risk, and market volatility.

5. Real estate crowdfunding: Real estate crowdfunding platforms allow multiple investors to pool their money together to invest in real estate projects.

(5-A) Real estate crowdfunding is a method of investing in real estate through online platforms that pool money from multiple investors to finance real estate projects. It is a relatively new concept that has gained popularity in recent years due to its accessibility and low investment minimums.

   - With real estate crowdfunding, investors can typically invest in a variety of real estate projects, including residential and commercial properties, as well as participate in various stages of the investment process, from ground-up development to refinancing.

   - One of the benefits of real estate crowdfunding is that it provides investors with a way to diversify their portfolio without needing to invest a large amount of money. Additionally, it allows investors to access deals that may have previously been available only to institutional investors or high net worth individuals.

   - However, it is important to note that real estate crowdfunding investments are generally considered higher risk and less liquid compared to traditional real estate investments, and investors should conduct thorough due diligence and carefully assess the risks involved before investing.

6. Vacation rental properties: Vacation rental properties, such as beach houses or cabins, can be rented out on a short-term basis to generate rental income.

  (6-A) Vacation rental properties are short-term rental properties that are typically rented out to travelers or vacationers looking for a temporary place to stay during their trip. Vacation rental properties can range from small apartments or condos to large vacation homes or villas.

   - One popular platform for listing vacation rental properties is Airbnb, which allows property owners to rent out their homes or apartments to travelers on a short-term basis. Other platforms include VRBO, HomeAway, and FlipKey.

- Investing in vacation rental properties can be a lucrative opportunity, as they can generate rental income during peak travel seasons.

- However, there are also challenges to consider, such as fluctuating demand, seasonal fluctuations in rental rates, and the need to manage the property remotely or hire a property management company.
- Additionally, there may be legal and regulatory requirements to comply with, such as obtaining the necessary permits and licenses to operate a vacation rental property in your area.

7. Real estate partnerships: Real estate partnerships involve pooling money with other investors to purchase and manage real estate properties.

(7-A) Real estate partnerships refer to the joining of two or more investors who pool their resources and knowledge to invest in real estate. In a partnership, each investor has a specific role and contributes a certain amount of capital to the investment. They share in the profits and losses of the investment, based on their agreed-upon percentage of ownership.

- Real estate partnerships can take various forms, including general partnerships, limited partnerships, and limited liability companies (LLCs). In a general partnership, all partners have equal management and liability responsibilities.

- In a limited partnership, there is at least one general partner who manages the investment and is personally liable for its obligations, and one or more limited partners who contribute capital but have limited management responsibilities and liability.

- Real estate partnerships can be a good option for investors who want to pool their resources and knowledge to invest in larger properties that they might not be able to afford on their own.

- Partnerships can also be a way to share the risks and rewards of real estate investing with others who have similar goals and values.

Each type of investment has its own unique benefits and risks, so it's important to carefully consider your goals, financial situation, and risk tolerance before choosing a real estate investment strategy. Additionally, working with experienced professionals, such as real estate agents, attorneys, and property managers, can help increase your chances of success.

Financing a real estate investment can be done through a variety of methods. Here are some common ways to finance a real estate investment:

1. Traditional mortgage loans: Traditional mortgage loans are the most common way to finance a real estate investment. These loans are typically available from banks and other lending institutions and require a down payment and a good credit score.

(1-A) A traditional mortgage loan is a type of home loan that is offered by banks, credit unions, and other financial institutions. It is used by borrowers to purchase a home, with the property serving as collateral for the loan.

- Under a traditional mortgage loan, the borrower makes regular monthly payments to the lender. These payments include both principal and interest, with the interest rate determined by the lender based on factors such as the borrower's credit score, income, and the current market conditions.

- Traditional mortgage loans typically require a down payment, which is a percentage of the home's purchase price paid upfront by the borrower. The down payment amount can vary, but is often around 20% of the purchase price.

   - One benefit of traditional mortgage loans is that they can offer competitive interest rates and long repayment terms, making homeownership more affordable for many borrowers.

   - However, they also come with the risk of foreclosure if the borrower is unable to make their payments.

Overall, traditional mortgage loans can be a good option for borrowers who have a stable income and credit history, and who are looking to buy a home as a long-term investment.

2. Hard money loans: Hard money loans are typically used for fix-and-flip properties or other short-term investments. These loans are provided by private lenders and often require higher interest rates and shorter repayment terms.

 (2-A) A hard money loan is a type of loan that is typically used for real estate investments, and is secured by the property being purchased. Unlike traditional mortgage loans, hard money loans are typically offered by private lenders or investors, rather than banks or other financial institutions.

   - Hard money loans are generally used by real estate investors who need to purchase properties quickly, as they typically have shorter loan terms and faster approval times than traditional mortgage loans.
   - However, they also typically have higher interest rates and fees than traditional loans, due to the increased risk associated with this type of lending.

- Because hard money loans are secured by the property being purchased, rather than the borrower's creditworthiness or other financial assets, lenders are primarily concerned with the value of the property and the borrower's ability to repay the loan.

- As a result, hard money loans are often a good option for real estate investors who have less-than-perfect credit, or who need to move quickly to take advantage of a particular investment opportunity.

3. Home equity loans or lines of credit: If you own a primary residence, you may be able to use a home equity loan or line of credit to finance a real estate investment. This can provide access to cash at a lower interest rate than other options.

(3-A) A home equity loan or line of credit is a type of loan that allows homeowners to borrow money against the equity they have built up in their home. Home equity is the difference between the current market value of the home and the outstanding balance on any mortgages or loans secured by the property.

- A home equity loan is a lump sum of money that is borrowed against the equity in the home and is repaid over a fixed term, typically with a fixed interest rate.

- Home equity lines of credit (HELOCs) are similar to credit cards, allowing homeowners to borrow against the equity in their home on an as-needed basis. HELOCs typically have a variable interest rate and a draw period during which borrowers can use the credit line, followed by a repayment period.

- Home equity loans and HELOCs can be used for a variety of purposes, including home improvements, debt consolidation, education expenses, and other major purchases.

- However, because the loans are secured by the home, there is a risk of foreclosure if the borrower fails to make payments.

4. Seller financing: Some real estate investors may be able to secure financing directly from the seller. This can involve the seller providing a loan for the purchase of the property or offering to hold a mortgage on the property.

(4-A) Seller financing, also known as owner financing, is a real estate financing option where the seller agrees to provide financing to the buyer instead of or in addition to traditional financing from a bank or other lender.

- In this arrangement, the seller acts as the lender and the buyer makes payments to the seller over time, typically with interest.

- This type of financing is often used when the buyer is unable to obtain traditional financing or when the seller wants to offer more flexible terms than those available through traditional financing options.

5. Private equity: Private equity firms or individuals may provide financing for real estate investments in exchange for a share of the profits.

(5-A) Private equity is a type of investment where capital is raised from high net worth individuals, institutional investors, and other sources to invest in private companies or take over public companies and make them private. Private equity firms typically use the funds they raise to buy a controlling interest in a company, improve its operations and financial performance, and then sell it at a profit.

- Private equity firms may also provide operational and management expertise to help companies grow and become more profitable. They may also use leverage, or borrowed money, to finance acquisitions or other activities.

- Investments in private equity can offer potentially high returns, but also carry significant risk. Investors typically commit their capital for a period of several years, during which time they may not have access to their funds.

- Private equity investments are generally illiquid, meaning that they cannot be easily bought or sold on a public exchange.

- Private equity investments can take many different forms, including leveraged buyouts, venture capital, growth equity, and distressed debt investing.

- The type of investment made will depend on the goals of the private equity firm and the needs of the company being invested in.

6. Crowdfunding: Real estate crowdfunding platforms may provide financing for real estate investments in exchange for a share of the profits.

(6-A) Crowdfunding is a method of raising capital through the collective effort of a large number of individuals, typically via the internet.

- In the context of investing, crowdfunding allows individuals to invest in a project or business and potentially earn a return on their investment.

- There are several types of crowdfunding, including equity-based crowdfunding, where investors receive equity or ownership in the company in exchange for their investment, and reward-based crowdfunding, where investors receive a non-financial reward, such as a product or service, in exchange for their investment.

- Crowdfunding has become an increasingly popular way for startups and small businesses to raise capital and for individual investors to diversify their portfolios.

- However, it is important to carefully research and evaluate any crowdfunding opportunity before investing to minimize the risk of losing your investment.

It's important to carefully consider the terms and risks associated with each financing option before making a decision. Additionally, working with an experienced real estate agent or attorney can help you navigate the financing process and ensure that you are making informed decisions.

Managing and growing a real estate portfolio involves several key steps, including:

1. Property management: If you own rental properties, effective property management is crucial to maintaining a profitable portfolio. This can involve tasks such as screening tenants, handling maintenance requests, and ensuring that rent is collected on time.

(1-A) Property management is the process of overseeing and maintaining real estate on behalf of the owner.

- This typically involves tasks such as finding and screening tenants, collecting rent, maintaining the property, handling repairs and maintenance, and ensuring compliance with local laws and regulations.

- Property management can be performed by the owner of the property themselves, or by a professional property management company that specializes in these tasks.

- The goal of property management is to maximize the value and profitability of the real estate investment, while minimizing the time and effort required by the owner.

2. Maintenance and repairs: Regular maintenance and repairs are necessary to keep properties in good condition and avoid costly repairs down the line. This can include tasks such as landscaping, cleaning, and repairs to plumbing, electrical, and HVAC systems.

(2-A) Maintenance and repairs are important aspects of managing a property. Regular maintenance helps keep the property in good condition and prevents minor issues from becoming major problems. This can save you time and money in the long run. It's also important to make repairs promptly to prevent further damage or potential safety hazards.

- Some common maintenance tasks include cleaning gutters, checking for leaks, changing air filters, and maintaining the HVAC system. You may also need to paint, replace flooring, or make other updates to keep the property in good condition.

- It's important to keep up with routine maintenance tasks and address any issues promptly to keep the property in good condition and maintain its value.

- When it comes to repairs, it's important to have a plan in place to handle them quickly and efficiently. You may want to have a list of reliable contractors and service providers you can call on when needed.

- It's also a good idea to have a budget set aside for repairs and maintenance so you can address any issues that arise without having to dip into your personal funds.

Overall, staying on top of maintenance and repairs is an important part of managing a property and can help ensure its long-term success.

3. Financial management: Proper financial management is crucial to ensuring that your real estate portfolio remains profitable. This can include tasks such as tracking income and expenses, creating budgets, and ensuring that rent is collected on time.

(3-A) Financial management in real estate investing involves keeping track of income, expenses, and profitability. It includes budgeting, accounting, and tax planning.

- To effectively manage your real estate investments, you should keep detailed records of all income and expenses, including rental income, mortgage payments, property taxes, insurance, maintenance and repair costs, and property management fees.

- This information can be tracked using software or spreadsheets, and it is important to review it regularly to ensure that you are staying within budget and maximizing profitability.

- Additionally, it is important to have a good understanding of tax laws and regulations related to real estate investments. You should work with a qualified accountant to ensure that you are taking advantage of all available tax deductions and credits.

- Finally, it is important to have a plan for reinvesting profits and managing cash flow. This may include saving for future investments, paying down debt, or creating a reserve fund for unexpected expenses.

- A solid financial management plan can help you to achieve long-term success in real estate investing.

4. Portfolio optimization: Over time, it may be necessary to adjust your real estate portfolio to optimize its performance. This can involve tasks such as selling underperforming properties, reinvesting profits into new properties, and diversifying your portfolio to minimize risk.

(4-A) Portfolio optimization is a process of selecting the best investment mix that meets an investor's financial goals while minimizing risk.

- The objective of portfolio optimization is to maximize the expected return of the portfolio while minimizing its risk.

- There are different approaches to portfolio optimization, but they generally involve selecting a combination of assets with different risk and return characteristics to achieve the desired risk-return profile.

- The process also involves continuous monitoring and rebalancing of the portfolio to ensure it stays aligned with the investor's goals and risk tolerance.

- Optimization can be done through various techniques such as mean-variance optimization, risk parity, and goal-based investing.

5. Networking and marketing: Building relationships with other real estate professionals and effectively marketing your properties can help you attract tenants, secure financing, and identify new investment opportunities.

(5-A) Networking and marketing are crucial for success in any industry, including real estate. Here are some tips for networking and marketing in the real estate industry:

- Attend industry events: Attend real estate conferences, seminars, and trade shows to meet other professionals in the industry, learn about new trends and technologies, and gain exposure for your business.

- Join industry associations: Join industry associations such as the National Association of Realtors or local real estate associations to gain access to networking opportunities, education, and industry resources.

- Build relationships with other professionals: Build relationships with other professionals in the industry, such as real estate agents, lenders, appraisers, and contractors, to establish a strong referral network.

- Leverage social media: Use social media platforms such as LinkedIn, Twitter, and Facebook to promote your business, share industry news and insights, and connect with other professionals in the industry.

- Create valuable content: Create valuable content such as blog posts, videos, and webinars that showcase your expertise and provide value to potential clients and other professionals in the industry.

- Build a strong brand: Develop a strong brand identity that reflects your business values, mission, and unique selling proposition. Use your brand to differentiate yourself from competitors and build trust with clients and partners.

- Attend local events: Attend local events such as charity functions, chamber of commerce meetings, and community events to meet potential clients and establish your presence in the local community.

6. Staying up-to-date on industry trends: The real estate industry is constantly evolving, so it's important to stay up-to-date on industry trends and changes in regulations that may impact your portfolio.

(6-A) Staying up-to-date on industry trends is essential for anyone working in a particular field. This is particularly true for real estate professionals, who must stay abreast of market trends, interest rates, economic conditions, and government regulations that can all impact the real estate market.

There are several ways to stay up-to-date on industry trends in real estate:

   - Attend industry events: Attending real estate conferences, trade shows, and seminars can provide valuable insights into the latest trends, best practices, and new technologies.

   - Follow industry publications: Real estate publications, such as Realtor Magazine, Real Estate Weekly, and HousingWire, can provide industry news, analysis, and expert opinions on market trends.

   - Network with peers: Networking with other real estate professionals can help you stay up-to-date on industry trends and best practices.

   - Follow industry leaders on social media: Many real estate leaders and experts are active on social media platforms like Twitter and LinkedIn, where they share insights, opinions, and updates on market trends.

- Take continuing education courses: Continuing education courses are a great way to stay current on industry trends and regulations while also earning credits for professional designations and licenses.

By staying up-to-date on industry trends, real estate professionals can make informed decisions, adapt to market changes, and provide the best possible service to their clients.

Effective management and growth of a real estate portfolio requires careful planning, attention to detail, and a willingness to adapt to changing market conditions. Working with experienced professionals, such as property managers, real estate agents, and attorneys, can help ensure that you are making informed decisions and optimizing the performance of your portfolio.

Chapter 6: Managing Risk and Protecting Your Wealth

Managing risk and protecting your wealth is an important part of any investment strategy. Here are some key steps to help you manage risk and protect your wealth:

1. Diversification: One of the most effective ways to manage risk is through diversification. This involves spreading your investments across different asset classes and sectors to reduce your exposure to any one particular investment.

(1-A) Diversification is a strategy that involves investing in a variety of different assets in order to reduce risk and increase potential returns.

- The idea behind diversification is that if one investment performs poorly, the losses can be offset by gains in other investments. By spreading your investments across different asset classes, sectors, and geographies, you can reduce the impact of any single event on your portfolio.

- Diversification can be achieved through a variety of investment vehicles, including stocks, bonds, mutual funds, exchange-traded funds (ETFs), real estate, commodities, and alternative investments.

- It is important to note that diversification does not guarantee a profit or protect against loss, but it can help to reduce overall portfolio risk.

- For example, if an investor only held stocks in the technology sector, their portfolio would be vulnerable to any negative events affecting the technology industry, such as a decline in consumer demand for tech products or new regulations that limit the industry's growth. By diversifying their portfolio to include other sectors such as healthcare, energy, and consumer goods, the investor can reduce the impact of any negative events on their overall portfolio.

2. Asset allocation: Determining the appropriate mix of assets for your portfolio can also help manage risk. This involves selecting investments with different levels of risk and return to create a well-balanced portfolio that aligns with your investment goals and risk tolerance.

(2-A) Asset allocation refers to the process of dividing an investment portfolio among different asset classes such as stocks, bonds, cash, and real estate, among others.

- The main objective of asset allocation is to balance risk and return by diversifying investments across various asset classes that are expected to behave differently in different market conditions.

- The idea behind asset allocation is to reduce the overall risk of the portfolio by spreading investments across a range of assets with different levels of volatility and expected returns.

- By doing so, investors can create a more stable portfolio that can withstand market fluctuations while providing the potential for long-term growth.

- Asset allocation is an important part of any investment strategy and should be done based on an investor's financial goals, risk tolerance, and time horizon.

3. Insurance: Insurance can help protect your assets from unexpected events such as natural disasters, accidents, or lawsuits. Common types of insurance for investors include property insurance, liability insurance, and umbrella policies.

(3-A) Insurance is a way of protecting yourself from financial loss in the event of an unforeseen event. In the context of investments, insurance can help to mitigate the risk of loss associated with certain types of investments.

- For example, you may choose to purchase insurance on your real estate investment to protect against damage or loss due to natural disasters or other unforeseen events.

- It is important to research and understand the different types of insurance available and to consult with a professional before making any insurance decisions.

- Some types of insurance that may be relevant to investment strategies include property and casualty insurance, liability insurance, and life insurance.

4. Estate planning: Developing an estate plan can help protect your wealth and ensure that your assets are distributed according to your wishes in the unfortunate event of your death. This can involve tasks such as creating a will, setting up trusts, and selecting beneficiaries for retirement accounts and life insurance policies.

(4-A) Estate planning involves the process of arranging for the transfer of a person's assets and wealth to their beneficiaries or heirs after their death.

- This process typically involves the creation of a will, which outlines how a person's assets will be distributed, and the designation of beneficiaries for insurance policies and retirement accounts.

- Estate planning can also involve the creation of trusts, which are legal entities that can hold and manage assets on behalf of beneficiaries.

- Trusts can be useful in situations where a person wants to leave assets to a minor child or to provide ongoing support to a loved one with special needs.

- Other components of estate planning may include the use of tax planning strategies to minimize the amount of taxes owed by the estate, the appointment of an executor or trustee to oversee the distribution of assets, and the designation of a power of attorney to make financial or medical decisions on behalf of the individual if they become incapacitated.

Estate planning is an important part of financial planning, and can help ensure that a person's assets are distributed according to their wishes and that their loved ones are taken care of after their death.

5. Regular monitoring and review: Regularly monitoring and reviewing your investments can help identify potential risks and ensure that your portfolio remains aligned with your goals and risk tolerance.

(5-A) Regular monitoring and review are crucial for successful financial planning. Even if you have a solid plan in place, it's important to review it on a regular basis to ensure that it still aligns with your goals and objectives, and to make adjustments as needed.

- A good rule of thumb is to review your financial plan at least once a year, or whenever there is a significant life event, such as a marriage, divorce, birth, or death.

- During the review process, you should evaluate your progress towards your goals, assess your risk tolerance, and make any necessary adjustments to your investment portfolio or other areas of your plan.

- It's also important to regularly monitor your accounts and investment performance to ensure that you are on track to meet your goals.

- This includes checking your account statements and tracking your progress towards savings goals.

- Regular monitoring and review can help you stay on track towards your financial goals and make adjustments as needed to ensure that you are taking the right steps to achieve financial success.

6. Working with financial professionals: Working with financial professionals such as financial advisors, attorneys, and tax professionals can help you identify and manage risks, develop an effective investment strategy, and ensure that your wealth is protected.

(6-A) Working with financial professionals can be helpful in managing your finances effectively. Some of the financial professionals that you may want to consider working with include:

- Financial advisor/planner: A financial advisor can help you create a comprehensive financial plan based on your goals and risk tolerance. They can also provide guidance on investment strategies and asset allocation.

- Accountant: An accountant can help you with tax planning and preparation, as well as other financial matters such as bookkeeping, budgeting, and financial statement analysis.

- Attorney: An attorney can help you with estate planning, including the creation of wills, trusts, and powers of attorney.

- Insurance agent: An insurance agent can help you evaluate your insurance needs and provide advice on the types of insurance coverage that may be appropriate for you.

- Real estate agent: A real estate agent can help you with buying or selling real estate, as well as provide advice on property management.

When choosing a financial professional, it's important to do your research and make sure they are qualified and reputable. Look for professionals who have relevant certifications and experience in their field. You may also want to check their credentials with professional organizations and regulatory bodies.

By taking a proactive approach to managing risk and protecting your wealth, you can help ensure that your investments continue to generate returns and provide financial security for you and your family.

Insurance is an important tool for managing risk and protecting your assets. Here is an overview of the most common types of insurance:

1. Life insurance: Life insurance provides a payout to your beneficiaries in the event of your death. There are two main types of life insurance: term life insurance, which provides coverage for a specified period of time, and permanent life insurance, which provides coverage for your entire life and may also include an investment component.

(1-A) Life insurance is a contract between an individual and an insurance company in which the insurer guarantees payment of a death benefit to the named beneficiaries upon the death of the insured.

- The insured pays a premium to the insurer in exchange for this protection. Life insurance is often used to provide financial support for loved ones in the event of the insured's death, to pay off debts or other expenses, and to help ensure the financial stability of dependents.

- There are different types of life insurance policies, such as term life, whole life, and universal life, each with their own features and benefits.

2. Health insurance: Health insurance provides coverage for medical expenses such as doctor visits, hospital stays, and prescription medications. There are several types of health insurance, including employer-sponsored plans, individual plans, and government programs such as Medicare and Medicaid.

(2-A) Health insurance is a type of insurance coverage that helps to pay for medical and surgical expenses incurred by the insured individual.

- Health insurance policies can be purchased by individuals or provided as a benefit by an employer. The cost of health insurance premiums can vary depending on factors such as the individual's age, health status, and the type of plan chosen.

- Health insurance plans can provide coverage for a variety of medical expenses, including doctor visits, hospital stays, prescription medications, and medical tests and procedures. Some plans may also offer coverage for dental and vision care.

3. Property insurance: Property insurance provides coverage for damage or loss to your property, including your home, car, or personal belongings. Common types of property insurance include homeowners insurance, renters insurance, and auto insurance.

(3-A) Property insurance is a type of insurance policy that provides financial protection to individuals or businesses in the event that their property is damaged, destroyed, or stolen.

- This type of insurance typically covers physical damage to the property, as well as liability for injuries or damage that occur on the property.

- Property insurance can cover a variety of assets, including homes, rental properties, commercial buildings, and personal belongings.

   - Some common types of property insurance include homeowners insurance, renters insurance, and commercial property insurance.

It's important to carefully consider your insurance needs and select the appropriate types and levels of coverage. Factors to consider include your age, health, occupation, and financial situation. Working with an experienced insurance agent or broker can help ensure that you have the right coverage in place to protect your assets and manage risk.

Estate planning is the process of preparing for the management and distribution of your assets after your death. Here are some of the most important tools for estate planning:

1. Wills: A will is a legal document that specifies how your assets will be distributed after your death. It can also name guardians for minor children and designate an executor to manage your estate.

 (1-A) A will is a legal document that outlines how a person's assets and possessions should be distributed after their death.

   - It allows you to name an executor, who is responsible for carrying out your wishes as stated in the will. Without a will, your assets will be distributed according to state laws, which may not align with your wishes.

   - When creating a will, you should consider your assets, debts, and beneficiaries. You may also want to name guardians for any minor children and provide instructions for your funeral arrangements.

- It's important to regularly review and update your will to ensure it remains current with your wishes and any changes in your life circumstances.

While it's possible to create a will on your own, it's often advisable to work with an attorney or other legal professional to ensure it's legally valid and covers all necessary details.

2. Trusts: A trust is a legal entity that can hold and manage assets for the benefit of beneficiaries. There are several types of trusts, including revocable living trusts, irrevocable trusts, and special needs trusts. Trusts can be used to avoid probate, minimize estate taxes, and provide ongoing management of assets for beneficiaries.

(2-A) A trust is a legal arrangement that allows a third party, or trustee, to hold assets on behalf of one or more beneficiaries.

- The trustee is responsible for managing the assets in the trust and distributing them to the beneficiaries according to the terms of the trust.

- Trusts can be used for a variety of purposes, such as to provide for minor children, to support a spouse or other family member, or to minimize estate taxes. There are many different types of trusts, each with its own set of rules and benefits.

- The most common types of trusts include revocable trusts, irrevocable trusts, testamentary trusts, and living trusts.

- A trust can be an effective tool for estate planning and asset protection, but it's important to work with an experienced attorney to set up the trust and ensure that it is managed properly.

3. Power of attorney: A power of attorney is a legal document that designates someone to act on your behalf if you become incapacitated. There are two main types of power of attorney: financial power of attorney, which allows someone to manage your financial affairs, and medical power of attorney, which allows someone to make medical decisions on your behalf.

(3-A) Power of attorney is a legal document that allows someone else to act on your behalf in financial, legal, or health-related matters.

- The person you designate as your agent, or attorney-in-fact, will have the legal authority to make decisions and take actions on your behalf if you become incapacitated or unable to make decisions for yourself.

- It is important to choose someone you trust as your agent and to carefully consider the scope of their authority.

- A power of attorney can be a valuable tool in estate planning and can provide peace of mind knowing that your affairs will be taken care of if you are unable to do so.

4. Beneficiary designations: Many types of assets, such as retirement accounts and life insurance policies, allow you to designate beneficiaries. These designations override any instructions in your will, so it's important to regularly review and update your beneficiary designations to ensure they reflect your current wishes.

(4-A) Beneficiary designations are a way to specify who will receive certain assets upon your death, without going through the probate process.

- Examples of assets that typically have beneficiary designations include life insurance policies, retirement accounts (such as 401(k)s and IRAs), and certain bank or investment accounts.

   - By designating beneficiaries, you can ensure that your assets are distributed according to your wishes and avoid potential conflicts or delays in the probate process.

   - It's important to periodically review your beneficiary designations to ensure they reflect your current wishes and that they are coordinated with your overall estate plan.

Estate planning can be complex, and it's important to work with an experienced estate planning attorney to ensure that your wishes are carried out and your assets are protected. By taking the time to develop an effective estate plan, you can provide peace of mind for yourself and your loved ones.

Investing always involves some degree of risk, but there are steps you can take to identify and manage those risks. Here are some key considerations for managing investment risks:

1. Asset allocation: Diversification is a key way to manage investment risk. By investing in a mix of assets such as stocks, bonds, and cash, you can reduce your exposure to any one type of investment.

 (1-A) Asset allocation is the process of dividing an investment portfolio among different asset classes, such as stocks, bonds, and cash, based on an investor's goals, risk tolerance, and investment time horizon.

   - The goal of asset allocation is to achieve a balance between risk and return by investing in a diversified mix of assets.

- A well-designed asset allocation strategy can help investors achieve their financial goals while minimizing risk.

- The optimal asset allocation depends on factors such as the investor's age, income, financial goals, and risk tolerance.

- It is important to regularly review and adjust the asset allocation to ensure it aligns with changing financial circumstances and market conditions.

2. Risk tolerance: Your risk tolerance is the degree of risk that you are comfortable taking on in your investments. It's important to understand your risk tolerance and invest accordingly.

(2-A) Risk tolerance refers to the level of financial risk that an individual or entity is willing and able to take.

- It is the degree of uncertainty that an investor can handle in regard to the potential loss or gain of an investment.

- Risk tolerance is subjective and varies based on individual circumstances such as financial goals, time horizon, income, and age.

- Investors with a higher risk tolerance are typically willing to invest in more volatile or risky investments with the potential for higher returns, while investors with a lower risk tolerance may prefer more conservative investments with lower returns but less volatility.

- It is important for investors to understand their risk tolerance and make investment decisions that align with their goals and comfort level.

3. Investment horizon: Your investment horizon is the length of time you plan to hold your investments. Generally, longer investment horizons can tolerate more risk than shorter investment horizons.

(3-A) Investment horizon refers to the length of time an investor plans to hold onto an investment before selling it.

- It is an important factor to consider when making investment decisions because different investments are more suitable for different investment horizons.

- For example, an investor with a short-term investment horizon may prefer to invest in more liquid assets like cash, money market funds or short-term bonds, whereas an investor with a long-term investment horizon may consider investing in assets with higher potential returns, such as stocks or real estate.

4. Investment research: Thoroughly research any investments you are considering, including their historical performance, fees, and risks.

(4-A) Investment research is the process of gathering and analyzing information about a particular investment or investment opportunity to make informed investment decisions.

- This information can include financial statements, economic data, market trends, company news and other relevant information.

- Investment research can be conducted by individual investors, professional money managers, or investment analysts who work for investment firms or financial institutions. The goal of investment research is to assess the potential risks and returns of an investment and to identify any potential opportunities or pitfalls.

- Some common methods of investment research include fundamental analysis, technical analysis, and quantitative analysis.

- Fundamental analysis involves evaluating a company's financial statements, management team, and competitive position to determine its potential for growth and profitability.

- Technical analysis involves analyzing market trends and patterns to identify potential entry and exit points for an investment.

- Quantitative analysis involves using mathematical models and statistical techniques to analyze investment opportunities.

- In addition to conducting research on individual investments, investors may also research broader market trends and economic indicators to help inform their investment decisions.

- This can include monitoring interest rates, inflation, and other macroeconomic factors that can affect the overall performance of different investment classes.

Overall, investment research is an important part of the investment process, helping investors make informed decisions and manage risk.

5. Monitoring and adjustments: Regularly monitor your investments to ensure they are performing as expected. If necessary, adjust your portfolio to better align with your investment goals and risk tolerance.

 (5-A) Monitoring and adjustments are crucial components of a successful investment strategy.

- Once you have established your investment plan, it is important to regularly review and analyze your portfolio to ensure that it aligns with your goals, risk tolerance, and time horizon.

- During the monitoring process, you should review the performance of your investments and assess whether any adjustments are necessary.

- This may involve rebalancing your portfolio to ensure that your asset allocation remains in line with your objectives, or making changes to your holdings based on new information or changing market conditions.

- It is also important to periodically review your investment plan to ensure that it remains appropriate for your current situation and goals.

- Life events such as marriage, children, or retirement can all impact your investment needs, and may require adjustments to your plan.

- Ultimately, regular monitoring and adjustments can help ensure that your investment strategy remains on track to help you achieve your financial goals.

- It is important to work with a financial advisor to develop an investment plan that is tailored to your individual needs and to establish a process for ongoing monitoring and adjustments.

6. Insurance: Insurance can be an important tool for managing investment risks. For example, property insurance can protect against damage to your rental properties, and disability insurance can provide income replacement in the event of a disability.

(6-A) Insurance is a financial product that provides protection against specific risks. In exchange for a premium, an insurance policy transfers the risk of financial loss from the insured individual or organization to the insurance company. There are various types of insurance products available, including:

   - Health insurance: Provides coverage for medical expenses incurred due to illness or injury.

   - Life insurance: Pays a benefit to designated beneficiaries upon the death of the insured.

   - Disability insurance: Provides income replacement in the event that the insured becomes disabled and unable to work.

   - Property insurance: Protects against damage or loss of physical property, such as a home or car.

   - Liability insurance: Provides coverage for damages or legal fees resulting from a lawsuit or other legal action.

Having insurance can help individuals and businesses mitigate financial risk and protect against unexpected events that could result in financial loss. It is important to carefully consider insurance needs and to review coverage regularly to ensure that it remains adequate and up-to-date.

By being proactive in managing investment risks, you can help ensure that your portfolio is well-positioned to meet your long-term investment goals.

Protecting your assets from creditors and lawsuits is an important consideration for wealth building. Here are some ways to protect your assets:

1. Insurance: Having adequate insurance coverage, such as liability insurance, can help protect you from financial loss in the event of a lawsuit.

(1-A) Yes, having adequate insurance coverage is an important aspect of personal finance and risk management.

- Liability insurance, in particular, can protect individuals and businesses from financial losses due to legal claims or lawsuits.

- Other types of insurance, such as health insurance, life insurance, disability insurance, and property insurance, can also provide valuable protection in the event of unexpected events or accidents.
- It's important to review your insurance coverage regularly to ensure that you have the right amount and type of coverage for your needs.

2. Entity formation: Consider forming a legal entity, such as a corporation or limited liability company (LLC), to hold your assets. This can provide a layer of protection between your personal assets and any business liabilities.

(2-A) Entity formation refers to the process of creating a legal entity for a business, such as a corporation, limited liability company (LLC), partnership, or sole proprietorship. The choice of entity depends on factors such as liability protection, taxation, and management structure.

- Incorporating a business as a corporation or LLC provides liability protection for the owners, which means that their personal assets are generally protected from business liabilities.

- Additionally, corporations and LLCs have a formal management structure, which can make it easier to raise capital and attract investors.

- Partnerships and sole proprietorships, on the other hand, are less formal business entities that do not provide liability protection for the owners.

- They are typically used for small businesses with a single owner or a few partners, and they are generally easier and less expensive to set up than corporations or LLCs.

When deciding on the type of entity to form, it's important to consult with legal and financial professionals to ensure that the chosen structure is appropriate for the business's needs and goals.

3. Trusts: Trusts can be used to hold assets and protect them from creditors. Irrevocable trusts, in particular, can provide strong asset protection.

(3-A) Trusts are legal arrangements that allow a trustee to hold and manage assets on behalf of a beneficiary or beneficiaries. The trustee has a fiduciary duty to manage the assets in the best interest of the beneficiary, according to the terms of the trust. Trusts can be used for various purposes, including estate planning, asset protection, and charitable giving.

There are many types of trusts, each with its own unique features and benefits. Some common types of trusts include:

- Revocable living trusts: A revocable living trust is a type of trust that is created during the grantor's lifetime and can be changed or revoked at any time. It is often used for estate planning purposes, as it allows the grantor to transfer assets to beneficiaries without going through probate.

- Irrevocable trusts: An irrevocable trust is a type of trust that cannot be changed or revoked once it has been created. It is often used for asset protection, as the assets in the trust are no longer considered to be owned by the grantor and are therefore protected from creditors.

- Charitable trusts: Charitable trusts are trusts that are set up for charitable purposes. They can provide tax benefits to the grantor while also supporting a charitable cause.

- Special needs trusts: Special needs trusts are trusts that are set up for the benefit of a person with special needs. They are designed to provide for the person's needs while also protecting their eligibility for government benefits.

- Testamentary trusts: Testamentary trusts are trusts that are created in a person's will and go into effect after the person's death. They are often used for estate planning purposes and can help ensure that assets are distributed according to the person's wishes.

It is important to work with a qualified attorney or financial advisor when setting up a trust to ensure that it is structured properly and meets your specific needs and goals.

4. Homestead exemption: In some states, a homestead exemption can protect your primary residence from creditors.

(4-A) A homestead exemption is a legal provision that protects the value of a homeowner's primary residence from certain creditors and property taxes.

- The exemption can vary by state and can provide homeowners with significant savings on their property taxes.

- In some states, a homestead exemption may also protect a portion of a homeowner's equity in the property from being seized by creditors to satisfy certain types of debts, such as credit card debt or medical bills.

It's important to check with your state's laws to determine if you qualify for a homestead exemption and the specific terms of the exemption.

5. Estate planning: Proper estate planning can help protect your assets from creditors and lawsuits. For example, setting up a trust or distributing assets through a will can help ensure that your assets are distributed according to your wishes and protected from creditors.

 (5-A) Estate planning is the process of arranging for the transfer of one's assets to their heirs or beneficiaries after their death.

   - It involves making decisions about who will inherit your assets, how they will inherit them, and when they will inherit them. The goal of estate planning is to ensure that your assets are distributed according to your wishes and that your loved ones are taken care of after your passing.

   - Some common estate planning tools include wills, trusts, and powers of attorney. A will is a legal document that outlines how your assets should be distributed after your death.

   - A trust is a legal arrangement in which a trustee manages your assets on behalf of your beneficiaries. Powers of attorney allow someone to make decisions on your behalf if you become incapacitated.

   - Other considerations in estate planning may include minimizing estate taxes, providing for charitable giving, and ensuring that your healthcare wishes are respected if you become unable to make decisions for yourself.

- It is important to work with an estate planning attorney to develop a plan that is tailored to your individual needs and circumstances. An estate planning attorney can help you understand the options available to you and ensure that your wishes are reflected in your estate plan.

It's important to consult with an attorney or financial advisor to determine the best strategies for protecting your assets from creditors and lawsuits based on your individual situation.

Chapter 7: Advanced Wealth Building Strategies

Once you have a solid foundation in place for building wealth, there are advanced strategies you can use to take your wealth building to the next level. Here are some advanced wealth building strategies to consider:

1. Tax planning: Advanced tax planning strategies can help you reduce your tax burden and maximize your after-tax income. These

strategies may include things like income splitting, tax-deferred investments, and capital gains tax planning.

(1-A) Tax planning involves the process of arranging your financial affairs in a way that minimizes your tax liability. This includes understanding tax laws and regulations, identifying tax deductions and credits, and developing a strategy to manage your taxes effectively.

- Tax planning can help individuals and businesses to save money on taxes, increase their after-tax income, and achieve their financial goals.

- There are several strategies that individuals and businesses can use to minimize their tax liability. Some of these strategies include:

- Deferring income: One strategy is to defer income until the following year, when tax rates may be lower. This can be achieved by deferring bonuses or other compensation until after the end of the tax year.

- Accelerating deductions: Another strategy is to accelerate deductions, such as charitable contributions or business expenses, into the current tax year to reduce taxable income.

- Maximizing retirement contributions: Contributing to tax-advantaged retirement accounts, such as a 401(k) or IRA, can reduce taxable income.

- Taking advantage of tax credits: Tax credits, such as the Earned Income Tax Credit or the Child Tax Credit, can help reduce your tax liability dollar-for-dollar.

- Structuring investments tax-efficiently: Structuring your investments in a tax-efficient manner, such as investing in tax-free municipal bonds, can help minimize your tax liability.

It's important to note that tax planning should not be confused with tax evasion, which is illegal. Tax evasion involves intentionally underreporting income or claiming false deductions in order to reduce tax liability.

2. Alternative investments: Alternative investments, such as hedge funds, private equity, and real estate syndications, can offer high potential returns but also come with higher risks. Consider consulting with a financial advisor to determine if these investments are suitable for your portfolio.

(2-A) Alternative investments are any investments that do not fit into the traditional categories of stocks, bonds, and cash.

- These investments can include a wide range of assets, such as real estate, commodities, hedge funds, private equity, and more.

- The primary benefit of alternative investments is their potential to provide diversification and reduce risk in an investment portfolio.

- However, they often come with higher fees, more complex structures, and less liquidity than traditional investments.

It is important for investors to carefully evaluate the risks and benefits of alternative investments and consider them in the context of their overall investment strategy.

3. Business ownership: Owning a business can provide significant opportunities for wealth building, but also comes with significant risks. Consider your risk tolerance and the potential rewards before pursuing business ownership.

(3-A) Business ownership involves owning a part or all of a business, and taking responsibility for its operation, profits, and losses.

   - There are several ways to own a business, including starting your own, buying an existing one, or investing in one as a partner or shareholder.

   - Business ownership can provide a source of income, build wealth, and offer the potential for long-term financial success.

   - However, it also involves risk, hard work, and the need for effective management and decision-making skills.

4. Philanthropy: Charitable giving can be an important component of advanced wealth building strategies, allowing you to support causes you care about while also potentially reducing your tax burden.

 (4-A) Philanthropy refers to the practice of giving money, time, or resources to charitable organizations or causes with the aim of improving the well-being of others or society as a whole.

   - Philanthropy can take many forms, including donating money to non-profit organizations, volunteering time and expertise, or supporting social and environmental initiatives.

   - There are many reasons why people engage in philanthropy, such as a desire to give back to their community, a sense of social responsibility, or a desire to create positive change in the world.

   - Additionally, philanthropy can provide a sense of personal fulfillment and satisfaction, as well as tax benefits in some cases.

   - Philanthropic giving can be done on an individual or organizational level, and there are many ways to get involved, such as donating to a favorite charity, starting a foundation or donor-advised fund, or participating in corporate social responsibility initiatives.

5. Estate planning: Advanced estate planning strategies, such as gifting, trust planning, and charitable giving, can help you maximize the transfer of your wealth to future generations while minimizing estate taxes.

(5-A) Advanced estate planning strategies involve more complex and sophisticated techniques to manage and distribute wealth. Some of the advanced estate planning strategies are:

- Generation-skipping trusts: These trusts are designed to provide assets for the benefit of future generations while minimizing or avoiding estate taxes.

- Charitable remainder trusts: These trusts allow individuals to make a gift to charity while retaining an income stream from the assets.

- Irrevocable life insurance trusts: These trusts allow individuals to remove life insurance proceeds from their taxable estate while still providing for their beneficiaries.

- Family limited partnerships: These partnerships allow families to pool assets and pass them on to the next generation while minimizing estate taxes.

- Grantor retained annuity trusts: These trusts allow individuals to transfer assets to their heirs at a reduced gift tax cost.

- Qualified personal residence trusts: These trusts allow individuals to transfer a residence to their heirs at a reduced gift tax cost.

It is important to consult with a qualified estate planning attorney and financial advisor to determine which advanced estate planning strategies are appropriate for your specific situation.

It's important to carefully consider the risks and rewards of any advanced wealth building strategies before pursuing them. Consult with a financial advisor or attorney to determine which strategies are best suited to your individual situation.

Alternative investments are non-traditional investments that are typically not available to the general public and often require a high degree of sophistication and expertise to understand and invest in. Some common types of alternative investments include hedge funds, private equity, real estate syndications, venture capital, and commodities.

1. Hedge funds: Hedge funds are investment funds that use a wide range of investment strategies to generate returns. They typically use a variety of financial instruments, such as derivatives and leverage, to enhance returns. Hedge funds are typically only available to accredited investors, who must meet certain income and net worth requirements.

 (1-A) Hedge funds are a type of investment vehicle that pools money from high net worth individuals and institutional investors and invests it in a variety of assets with the goal of generating high returns.
   - Hedge funds typically use more aggressive investment strategies than traditional investments, such as short-selling, leverage, and derivatives.

- They are generally only available to accredited investors due to their high minimum investment requirements and limited regulatory oversight.

2. Private equity: Private equity refers to investments in private companies or businesses that are not publicly traded. Private equity funds are typically used to invest in companies that are in need of growth capital or restructuring. Private equity investments are typically illiquid and require a long-term commitment from investors.

(2-A) Private equity refers to investments made in private companies or assets that are not publicly traded.

- Private equity firms invest directly in these companies, usually with the aim of improving their operations and increasing their value, before selling their stake at a profit.

- Private equity investments typically require large amounts of capital and are generally considered high-risk, high-reward investments.

- Private equity can be a way for investors to gain exposure to businesses that are not accessible through public markets, and it can be an important source of capital for companies that are looking to expand or restructure.

- However, due to the complex and often opaque nature of private equity investments, they are generally only available to accredited investors and institutional investors.

3. Real estate syndications: Real estate syndications are a way for individual investors to pool their money together to invest in real estate. This can be a way to invest in larger, more complex real

estate projects that would be difficult or impossible to invest in as an individual.

(3-A) Real estate syndication is a way for a group of investors to pool their resources and collectively invest in real estate projects.

- In a real estate syndication, there is typically one or more experienced real estate professionals who manage the project and find the deals, while the investors provide the capital.

- Real estate syndications can take many forms, but the most common structure is a limited liability company (LLC) where the sponsor (the real estate professional) is the managing member and the investors are passive members.

- The LLC agreement sets out the terms of the syndication, including the investment terms, the responsibilities of the sponsor and the rights of the investors.

- Real estate syndications can offer investors several benefits, including the ability to invest in larger and more complex deals than they could on their own, access to the expertise of experienced real estate professionals, and the potential for higher returns than traditional investments.

- However, like any investment, there are also risks to consider, such as the possibility of losing money or the lack of liquidity.

4. Venture capital: Venture capital refers to investments in early-stage companies with high growth potential. Venture capital firms typically invest in companies that are not yet profitable and may be several years away from going public.

(4-A) Venture capital (VC) is a type of private equity investment that typically involves providing funding to early-stage, high-growth companies with the potential for significant returns.

- VC firms pool money from investors, such as wealthy individuals, institutional investors, and corporations, and use that capital to invest in startups and other emerging companies.

- In exchange for their investment, VC firms typically receive equity in the company, meaning they own a percentage of the company's stock.

- They may also have a seat on the company's board of directors and provide strategic guidance and other support to help the company grow.

- VC investments can be risky, as many startups fail and investors may not receive a return on their investment.

- However, successful VC investments can generate substantial returns, with some startups going public or being acquired for billions of dollars.

- VC investing is typically only available to accredited investors, who are individuals with a high net worth or income and institutions that meet certain financial requirements.

5. Commodities: Commodities are raw materials or primary agricultural products that are traded on commodity exchanges. Commodities can include things like gold, silver, oil, and agricultural products.

(5-A) Commodities are physical goods or raw materials that are used in commerce, such as oil, gold, wheat, or natural gas.

- They are often traded on exchanges, and their prices can be highly volatile due to changes in supply and demand, geopolitical events, and other factors.

- Investing in commodities can provide diversification benefits and may be used as a hedge against inflation or other economic risks.

- There are several ways to invest in commodities, including buying physical commodities, trading commodity futures contracts, or investing in exchange-traded funds (ETFs) that track commodity prices.
- It's important to note that investing in commodities can be risky and may not be suitable for all investors, as prices can be highly unpredictable and affected by a wide range of factors.

It's important to note that alternative investments often come with higher risks and may not be suitable for all investors. It's important to consult with a financial advisor to determine if alternative investments are appropriate for your investment portfolio.

Tax planning and optimization is an important aspect of wealth building. By minimizing the amount of taxes you pay, you can maximize the amount of money you keep and invest. Here are some key strategies for tax planning and optimization:

1. Understanding tax brackets: Understanding the tax brackets and rates can help you plan your income and investments in a way that minimizes your tax liability.

(1-A) Tax brackets are the ranges of taxable income in which different tax rates are applied to determine the amount of tax owed to the government.

- In the United States, the federal government uses a progressive tax system with seven different tax brackets ranging from 10% to 37%.

- The tax bracket you fall into depends on your taxable income, which is calculated by subtracting deductions and exemptions from your gross income.

-The seven tax brackets for the 2023 tax year (for single filers) are as follows:

10% for taxable income up to $10,275
12% for taxable income over $10,275 up to $42,525
22% for taxable income over $42,525 up to $110,500
24% for taxable income over $110,500 up to $205,500
32% for taxable income over $205,500 up to $409,600
35% for taxable income over $409,600 up to $418,400
37% for taxable income over $418,400

It's important to note that the tax rates and income thresholds can change from year to year, and they can also be different for married filing jointly, married filing separately, and head of household tax filers.

2. Maximizing retirement contributions: Contributing to retirement accounts, such as 401(k)s and IRAs, can help you reduce your taxable income while saving for the future.

(2-A) Maximizing retirement contributions can be a smart strategy to save for retirement and reduce your current tax liability.

- There are several types of retirement accounts available, including traditional IRAs, Roth IRAs, 401(k)s, and other employer-sponsored plans. Each type of account has its own contribution limits and tax advantages.

- For example, traditional IRA contributions may be tax-deductible, while Roth IRA contributions are made with after-tax dollars but offer tax-free withdrawals in retirement.

- 401(k) contributions may be made on a pre-tax basis, reducing your taxable income, and some employers may match a portion of your contributions.

- To maximize your retirement contributions, you'll need to contribute the maximum allowed amount to each account type. For 2022, the contribution limit for traditional and Roth IRAs is $6,000, or $7,000 if you're 50 or older.

- The contribution limit for 401(k)s is $20,500, or $27,000 if you're 50 or older.

It's important to note that contribution limits can change from year to year, so be sure to stay up-to-date on the latest rules and regulations. Additionally, it's always a good idea to consult with a financial professional to determine the best retirement savings strategy for your individual needs and goals.

3. Taking advantage of tax deductions and credits: There are a variety of tax deductions and credits available that can reduce your tax liability, such as deductions for charitable donations, mortgage interest, and state and local taxes.

(3-A) There are a number of tax deductions and credits that can help reduce your tax liability, including:

- Retirement contributions: Contributions to certain retirement accounts, such as traditional IRAs or 401(k)s, can be deducted from your taxable income.

- Charitable donations: Donations to qualified charitable organizations can be deductible, up to a certain limit based on your income.

- Mortgage interest: If you own a home and have a mortgage, you can deduct the interest paid on the loan from your taxable income.

- Education expenses: Certain education expenses, such as tuition and student loan interest, can be deductible.

- Medical expenses: If your medical expenses exceed a certain percentage of your income, you may be able to deduct them from your taxable income.

- State and local taxes: You can deduct state and local income, sales, and property taxes up to a certain limit.

- Earned Income Tax Credit (EITC): This credit is available to low- to moderate-income individuals and families.

It's important to consult with a tax professional to determine which deductions and credits are applicable to your specific situation.

4. Tax-loss harvesting: Tax-loss harvesting involves selling investments that have decreased in value to offset gains in other investments, reducing your overall tax liability.

(4-A) Tax-loss harvesting is a tax strategy used by investors to reduce their tax liability by selling assets that have experienced losses and using those losses to offset gains in other investments.

- This can be especially useful for investors who have realized capital gains on investments during the year and want to minimize their tax liability.

- For example, if an investor sold a stock for a $5,000 capital gain, they would owe taxes on that gain. However, if they had also sold a different stock that had lost $5,000, they could use that loss to offset the gain and reduce their tax liability.

- It is important to note that there are rules and limitations surrounding tax-loss harvesting, such as the wash-sale rule, which prevents investors from buying a "substantially identical" asset within 30 days of selling the loss-generating asset.

- It is also important to consider the long-term investment strategy before selling assets solely for the purpose of harvesting losses.

5. Using tax-advantaged accounts: There are a variety of tax-advantaged accounts, such as Health Savings Accounts (HSAs) and 529 college savings plans, that can provide tax benefits and help you save for specific financial goals.

(5-A) Tax-advantaged accounts are financial accounts that offer tax benefits to the account holder. These accounts can be used to save for retirement or for other purposes, such as education or medical expenses. Some common types of tax-advantaged accounts include:

- 401(k) plans: These are employer-sponsored retirement plans that allow employees to make tax-deductible contributions to their retirement savings. Contributions and investment earnings grow tax-free until they are withdrawn, at which point they are taxed as income.

- Traditional IRAs: These are individual retirement accounts that allow individuals to make tax-deductible contributions to their retirement savings. Contributions and investment earnings grow tax-free until they are withdrawn, at which point they are taxed as income.

- Roth IRAs: These are individual retirement accounts that allow individuals to make after-tax contributions to their retirement savings. Contributions and investment earnings grow tax-free and are not subject to taxes when withdrawn in retirement.

- Health savings accounts (HSAs): These accounts are used to save for medical expenses and offer tax benefits to those who qualify. Contributions are tax-deductible, investment earnings grow tax-free, and withdrawals for qualified medical expenses are tax-free.

- 529 college savings plans: These accounts are used to save for education expenses and offer tax benefits to those who qualify. Contributions are not tax-deductible, but investment earnings grow tax-free and withdrawals for qualified education expenses are tax-free.

6. Consulting with a tax professional: Working with a tax professional can help you identify strategies to minimize your tax liability and ensure that you are in compliance with tax laws and regulations.

(6-A) Consulting with a tax professional can be helpful in ensuring that you are taking advantage of all available tax strategies and minimizing your tax liability.

- A tax professional can provide advice and guidance on tax planning, as well as help you prepare and file your tax returns accurately and on time. They can also represent you in case of an audit or other tax-related issues.

- It is important to choose a qualified and experienced tax professional who has a good reputation and is familiar with your specific tax situation.

It's important to note that tax laws and regulations can change frequently, so it's important to stay up-to-date on the latest developments and consult with a tax professional before making any major financial decisions.

Maximizing retirement savings is a crucial aspect of wealth building. Here are some key strategies for maximizing retirement savings:

1. Contributing to a 401(k): A 401(k) is a tax-advantaged retirement savings account that is offered by many employers. Contributions to a 401(k) are made on a pre-tax basis, which can help reduce your taxable income while saving for retirement.

(1-A) A 401(k) is a retirement savings plan sponsored by an employer. It allows employees to contribute a portion of their pre-tax income to the plan, and the contributions grow tax-free until they are withdrawn in retirement. Many employers also offer a matching contribution, which can help boost your savings.

   - Contributing to a 401(k) is a great way to save for retirement while also reducing your taxable income. For 2023, the maximum employee contribution to a 401(k) is $20,500, and individuals over age 50 can make an additional $6,500 catch-up contribution.

   - However, keep in mind that there may be penalties for withdrawing funds from your 401(k) before age 59 and a half, so it's important to consider your long-term financial goals before making contributions.
   - Additionally, you should review your investment options within your 401(k) to ensure that they align with your risk tolerance and retirement goals.

2. Contributing to an IRA: An Individual Retirement Account (IRA) is another type of tax-advantaged retirement savings account. There are two main types of IRAs: traditional and Roth. Contributions to a traditional IRA are tax-deductible, while contributions to a Roth IRA are made on an after-tax basis.

(2-A) Individual Retirement Accounts (IRAs) are a type of retirement account that individuals can contribute to on their own, regardless of whether they have a workplace retirement plan or not.

- There are two main types of IRAs: Traditional IRAs and Roth IRAs. Traditional IRAs offer tax-deferred growth, which means that the contributions are tax-deductible in the year they are made, and the earnings grow tax-free until you withdraw the money in retirement.

- Roth IRAs, on the other hand, do not offer an immediate tax deduction, but the earnings and withdrawals in retirement are tax-free.

- Both types of IRAs have contribution limits set by the IRS each year. For 2023, the contribution limit is $6,000 for those under age 50 and $7,000 for those 50 and older.

- There are also income limits for contributions to a Roth IRA. For 2023, single taxpayers with modified adjusted gross incomes (MAGI) of $140,000 or more and married couples filing jointly with MAGIs of $208,000 or more are not eligible to contribute to a Roth IRA.

- However, they can still contribute to a traditional IRA, although the contributions may not be tax-deductible depending on their income and whether they have a workplace retirement plan.

3. Taking advantage of employer matching: Many employers offer matching contributions to 401(k) plans, which can help you save more for retirement. Be sure to contribute enough to your 401(k) to receive the full employer match.

(3-A) Employer matching is a benefit some companies offer their employees as an incentive to contribute to a retirement plan, such as a 401(k).

- With employer matching, the company will match a certain percentage of the employee's contribution up to a certain limit. For example, an employer might match 50% of an employee's contributions up to 6% of their salary.

- It is important to take advantage of employer matching if it is offered because it is essentially free money. By contributing at least enough to meet the employer match, employees can increase their retirement savings without having to contribute additional funds themselves.

4. Catch-up contributions: If you are age 50 or older, you can make additional "catch-up" contributions to your retirement accounts to help you save more for retirement.

(4-A) Catch-up contributions are extra contributions that individuals aged 50 and over can make to certain retirement accounts above and beyond the regular contribution limits.

- These contributions are designed to help those who are closer to retirement age save more money in a shorter amount of time.

- For example, in 2023, individuals aged 50 or older can contribute an additional $1,000 to traditional or Roth IRAs, on top of the annual contribution limit of $6,000, for a total contribution of $7,000.

- Similarly, individuals aged 50 or older can contribute an additional $6,500 to a 401(k) plan on top of the annual contribution limit of $19,500, for a total contribution of $26,000.

- It's important to note that catch-up contributions are not available for all types of retirement accounts, so it's important to check with the specific plan or account to see if this option is available.

5. Consider a SEP or SIMPLE IRA: If you are self-employed or a small business owner, a Simplified Employee Pension (SEP) or Savings Incentive Match Plan for Employees (SIMPLE) IRA may be a good option for maximizing retirement savings.

(5-A) Yes, a Simplified Employee Pension (SEP) IRA or Savings Incentive Match Plan for Employees (SIMPLE) IRA can be a good option for self-employed individuals or small business owners to save for retirement.

- A SEP IRA allows employers to make tax-deductible contributions on behalf of eligible employees, including themselves, up to 25% of their compensation or a maximum contribution of $59,000 for 2021.

- A SIMPLE IRA allows both employers and employees to make contributions, with employer contributions being either a dollar-for-dollar match of up to 3% of an employee's salary or a non-elective contribution of 2% of an employee's salary.

- Employees can also contribute up to $13,500 for 2021, with a catch-up contribution of an additional $3,000 allowed for those over age 50.

- Both SEP and SIMPLE IRAs offer tax-deferred growth and can be a good option for small business owners looking for a relatively easy way to provide retirement benefits to themselves and their employees.

- However, it's important to carefully consider the contribution limits and other requirements associated with each type of IRA to determine which one is best suited for your specific situation.

6. Consult with a financial advisor: A financial advisor can help you identify strategies for maximizing retirement savings and ensure that you are on track to meet your retirement goals.

(6-A) Consulting with a financial advisor can be a helpful step in creating a personalized plan for retirement savings.

- A financial advisor can assess your current financial situation, help you identify your retirement goals, and recommend strategies to achieve those goals.

- They can also help you navigate the complex world of retirement accounts, including tax-advantaged accounts like 401(k)s and IRAs.

- Additionally, a financial advisor can provide guidance on investment choices, asset allocation, and risk management to help ensure that your retirement savings are on track.

- It's important to choose a financial advisor who is a fiduciary, meaning that they are legally obligated to act in your best interests.

It's important to start saving for retirement as early as possible and to make regular contributions to your retirement accounts. By maximizing your retirement savings, you can help ensure that you have enough money to support yourself in retirement and achieve your long-term financial goals.

Philanthropy and giving back is an important aspect of wealth building. Here are some key ways to give back:

1. Donating to charity: Charitable donations can help support important causes and organizations. Consider donating to charities that align with your values and priorities.

(1-A) Donating to charity is a great way to give back to your community while also receiving tax benefits.

- When you donate to a qualified charitable organization, you may be able to deduct the value of your donation from your taxable income.

- There are many ways to donate to charity, including donating cash, appreciated assets such as stocks or real estate, and even donating your time through volunteering.

- It's important to do your research and choose a reputable charity that aligns with your values and goals.

- Keep in mind that there are limits to how much you can deduct for charitable donations, and the rules can be complex. It may be beneficial to consult with a tax professional or financial advisor to determine the best way to structure your donations for maximum tax benefits.

2. Volunteerism: Giving back doesn't always have to involve money. Consider volunteering your time and skills to support local organizations or causes.

(2-A) Volunteerism refers to the act of offering one's time and skills to help others without any expectation of payment or reward.

- It is a way to contribute to society, make a difference, and gain personal fulfillment. Volunteer opportunities can range from serving at a local soup kitchen to tutoring disadvantaged children, assisting in disaster relief efforts, or participating in a community service project.

 - Many individuals and organizations engage in volunteerism as a way to promote social causes, support their local communities, or advance personal growth and development.

3. Setting up a family foundation: Setting up a family foundation can provide a structured way to give back and involve multiple generations of your family in philanthropy.

(3-A) Setting up a family foundation is a great way to support charitable causes while also providing a lasting legacy for your family. Here are some steps to consider:

 - Determine the mission and purpose of the foundation: Decide what causes and organizations the foundation will support and what its goals and objectives are.

 - Choose a name and structure for the foundation: Decide on a name for the foundation and choose a structure that best fits your goals and objectives. The most common types of foundations are private foundations and donor-advised funds.

 - Create a governing document: The governing document outlines the structure, purpose, and governance of the foundation. It should include provisions for how the foundation will operate, how grants will be awarded, and how the board of directors will be appointed and operate.

- Obtain tax-exempt status: To receive tax-exempt status, you will need to file articles of incorporation and apply for tax-exempt status with the IRS.

- Appoint a board of directors: The board of directors is responsible for managing the foundation and making decisions about grants and other activities.

- Establish policies and procedures: Establish policies and procedures for the foundation to ensure that it operates in compliance with all applicable laws and regulations.

- Fund the foundation: Once the foundation is established, you can fund it with cash, securities, or other assets.

- Manage the foundation: Manage the foundation and make grants to organizations that further its mission and purpose.

4. Impact investing: Impact investing involves making investments in companies or organizations that align with your values and priorities, with the goal of generating both social and financial returns.

(4-A) Impact investing refers to investments made with the intention of generating positive, measurable social and environmental impact, as well as a financial return.

- Impact investors seek to support companies and organizations that are working to create positive social or environmental change while also generating financial returns for investors.

- Examples of impact investments include investing in companies that provide affordable housing, clean energy, or education opportunities, among others.

- The impact investing industry has grown significantly in recent years, driven by increasing interest among investors in aligning their investments with their values and a desire to make a positive difference in the world.

5. Donor-advised funds: A donor-advised fund is a charitable giving vehicle that allows you to make contributions to the fund and recommend grants to charities of your choice over time.

(5-A) A donor-advised fund (DAF) is a charitable giving vehicle that allows individuals, families, and organizations to make a charitable contribution to a sponsoring organization, such as a community foundation or financial institution, and receive an immediate tax deduction. The donor then recommends how the funds are to be distributed to specific charitable organizations over time.

- Donor-advised funds offer several benefits, including simplified record-keeping and administrative tasks compared to establishing a private foundation, as well as flexibility in making charitable donations.

- Donors can contribute a wide range of assets, including cash, appreciated securities, and other assets, and can recommend grants to any qualified charitable organization, including public charities, private foundations, and religious organizations.

- Additionally, donor-advised funds allow for philanthropic giving to be spread out over time, giving donors the opportunity to make strategic decisions about their giving and support causes they are passionate about.

6. Estate planning: Estate planning can provide an opportunity to leave a legacy by including charitable giving in your will or estate plan.

(6-A) Estate planning is the process of anticipating and arranging for the management and disposal of an individual's assets in the event of their incapacitation or death.

- Estate planning typically involves creating a will, establishing trusts, and designating beneficiaries for assets such as life insurance policies and retirement accounts.

- The goal of estate planning is to ensure that an individual's assets are distributed according to their wishes, and that their loved ones are provided for in the event of their passing. Effective estate planning can also help to minimize taxes and other costs associated with the transfer of assets.

- It is important to regularly review and update your estate plan as your life circumstances change.

By giving back and supporting causes that are important to you, you can help make a positive impact on the world and create a sense of purpose and fulfillment. It's important to approach philanthropy and giving back in a thoughtful and intentional way, and to work with a financial advisor or other professionals to ensure that your giving aligns with your overall financial plan.

Chapter 8: Conclusion: Putting it All Together

In conclusion, building wealth is a journey that requires discipline, hard work, and a long-term perspective. By assessing your current financial situation, setting goals, creating a budget, saving and investing for the future, considering entrepreneurship and real estate investing, managing risk, and giving back through philanthropy, you can develop a comprehensive wealth building strategy that helps you achieve your financial goals.

It's important to remember that wealth building is not a one-size-fits-all approach, and what works for one person may not work for another. However, by understanding the key principles and strategies outlined in this book and working with a trusted financial advisor, you can develop a plan that is tailored to your unique situation and priorities.

Remember that building wealth is a marathon, not a sprint, and it's important to stay disciplined and committed to your plan over the long term. By taking control of your financial future and building wealth over time, you can create a more secure and fulfilling life for yourself and those you care about.

Here are some key takeaways from this book on wealth building:

1. Building wealth is important because it can help you achieve financial independence and provide more opportunities and security for yourself and your loved ones.

2. To start building wealth, it's important to assess your current financial situation, set financial goals, create a budget, and save and invest for the future.

3. You can consider entrepreneurship and real estate investing as alternative wealth building strategies, but it's important to understand the risks involved.

4. Managing risk is a crucial part of wealth building, and you can do this by having the right insurance policies, estate planning, and asset protection strategies.

5. Advanced wealth building strategies like alternative investments and tax planning can help you optimize your portfolio and maximize returns.

6. Giving back through philanthropy can be a fulfilling way to make a positive impact on the world while also supporting your financial goals.

7. Wealth building is a long-term journey that requires discipline, commitment, and a solid plan tailored to your unique situation and priorities.

An important takeaway from this book on wealth building is the importance of ongoing learning and financial education. Building wealth is a complex process, and it's important to stay up-to-date with the latest trends, best practices, and investment opportunities to make informed decisions and maximize your returns.

By continuing to educate yourself through books, articles, seminars, and working with trusted financial advisors, you can develop a deeper understanding of the financial landscape and make informed decisions that align with your financial goals and risk tolerance.

Additionally, financial education can help you avoid common pitfalls and mistakes that can derail your wealth building journey, such as excessive debt, overspending, and lack of diversification. By staying informed and educated, you can build a more secure and fulfilling financial future for yourself and those you care about.

Finally, it's important to note that building wealth is a journey that starts with taking action. While it can seem overwhelming at first, the key is to start small and build momentum over time. By taking small steps like creating a budget, setting financial goals, and automating your savings, you can start building the habits and behaviors that will lead to long-term financial success.

Remember, building wealth is not a sprint, it's a marathon. It takes time, discipline, and patience. But by starting today, you'll be on your way to achieving financial independence and creating the life you've always dreamed of. So don't wait, take action and start building wealth today!

Written & Illustrated By:
- Zachary Davis Sr.

www.ingramcontent.com/pod-product-compliance
Lightning Source LLC
Chambersburg PA
CBHW020422220526
45464CB00002B/529